the best of
CROSS STITCH BASICS

BIBS • **FLORALS** • **SAMPLERS** • **BOOKMARKS** • **ALPHABETS**

LEISURE ARTS, INC.
Little Rock, Arkansas

EDITORIAL STAFF

Editor-in-Chief: Susan White Sullivan
Designer Relations Director: Debra Nettles
Craft Publications Director: Cheryl Johnson
Special Projects Director: Susan Frantz Wiles
Senior Prepress Director: Mark Hawkins
Technical Writer: Frances Huddleston
Technical Associates: Laura Bertram and
    Mary Sullivan Hutcheson
Editorial Writer: Susan McManus Johnson
Art Publications Director: Rhonda Shelby
Art Category Manager: Lora Puls
Lead Graphic Artist: Janie Marie Wright
Graphic Artists: Dayle Carozza, Jacob Casleton,
    Angela Ormsby Stark, and Amy Temple
Imaging Technicians: Brian Hall,
    Stephanie Johnson, and Mark R. Potter
Photography Manager: Katherine Laughlin
Contributing Photographer: Ken West
Contributing Photostylist: Christy Myers
Publishing Systems Administrator:
    Becky Riddle
Publishing Systems Assistant: Clint Hanson
Mac IT Specialist: Robert Young

BUSINESS STAFF

Vice President and Chief Operations Officer:
    Tom Siebenmorgen
Director Of Finance and Administration:
    Laticia Mull Dittrich
Vice President, Sales And Marketing:
    Pam Stebbins
Sales Director: Martha Adams
Marketing Director: Margaret Reinold
Creative Services Director: Jeff Curtis
Information Technology Director: Hermine Linz
Controller: Francis Caple
Vice President, Operations: Jim Dittrich
Comptroller, Operations: Rob Thieme
Retail Customer Service Manager: Stan Raynor
Print Production Manager: Fred F. Pruss

Library of Congress Control Number: 2010923136
ISBN-13: 978-1-60140-992-8
ISBN-10: 1-60140-992-3

table of CONTENTS

Bibs .... pages 4-17

Florals .... pages 18-43

Samplers .... pages 44-71

Bookmarks .... pages 72-82

Alphabets .... pages 83-92

General Instructions .. pages 93-96

75

88

19

51

5

At Leisure Arts, we're excited to present 108 of our classic Cross Stitch designs by such popular artists as Lynn Waters Busa, Jane Chandler, Deborah A. Lambein, and Paula Vaughan. Why not stitch the sweet samplers and floral pillows to refresh your home? You can embellish the most adorable bibs for a baby shower. Or give your favorite reader the perfect bookmark. In fact, there are lots of fun surprises to make for friends, including mini samplers, needle cases, and scented sachets. Plus, you'll find a huge variety of alphabets to personalize your work or fashion your own original sayings! Photos, color charts, and easy instructions—96 pages in all—will provide endless hours of Cross Stitch creativity!

There's no doubting which babies wear the Beary Cute Bibs, because little bears point to their cross-stitched names. Everyone loves Baby, including the happy elephants, bears, and pigs on the Animal Bibs. Why not record the daily activities of that wee person on a Baby Talk bib? You'll also enjoy celebrating the arrival of a long-awaited infant with Marching Ducks and Bunny Flowers tie-on bibs.

Charts on pages 10-13.

Baby won't have to fish for compliments while wearing any of the three "Dino-mite" Bibs. Stitched with familiar chubby shapes and lovable faces, the Panda bib and towel are also crowd pleasers. Inspired by old-fashioned patchwork, Calico Bibs tell it like it is—in cross stitch!

Charts on pages 13-15.

Whether your tyke is a Candy Cane Kid or a big fan of Santa, you can keep his or her cute holiday outfits looking fresh with these Christmas Bibs. Want to hear your baby shower gift get plenty of "oohs" and "aahs"? Little Girls and Boys are a clever set that welcomes the new arrival with a traditional rhyme.

Charts on pages 16-17.

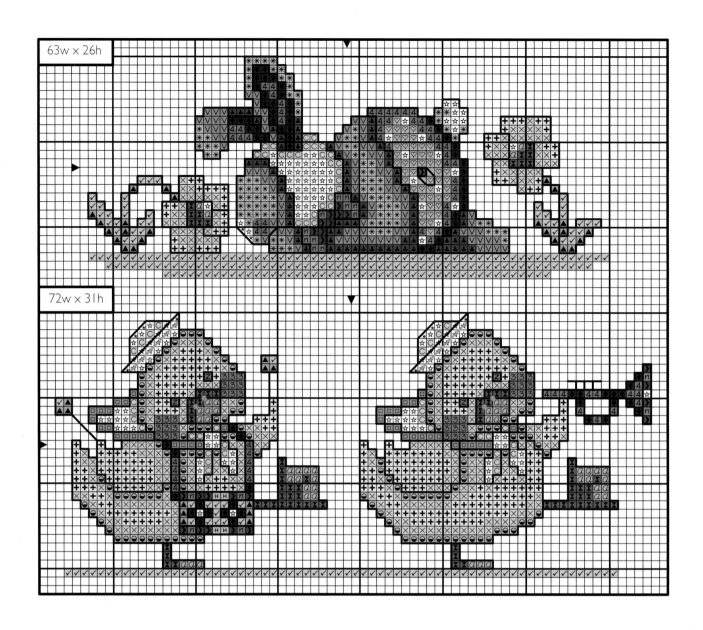

X	DMC	1/4X	COLOR
☆	blanc	◹	white
▶	208		dk purple
n	209		purple
H	210		lt purple
Z	312		dk blue
▙	436		dk tan
V	437		tan
▲	562		green

X	DMC	COLOR
✔	563	lt green
◆	602	dk pink
4	603	pink
♡	605	lt pink
✳	739	lt tan
✕	740	orange
a	741	lt orange
◗	743	dk yellow

X	DMC	B'ST	COLOR
✕	744		yellow
➕	745		lt yellow
3	760		salmon
C	775		lt blue
▢	798	╱	blue
	3371	╱	black brown
●	3371		black brown Fr. Knot

BUNNY FLOWERS and MARCHING DUCKS (shown on page 5) were stitched on Aida (14 ct) infant bibs. Three strands of floss were used for Cross Stitch and 1 strand for Backstitch and Fr. Knots. Design sizes are 4½" x 1⅞" (Bunny Flowers) and 5¼" x 2¼" (Marching Ducks).

Designs by Lorrie Birmingham.

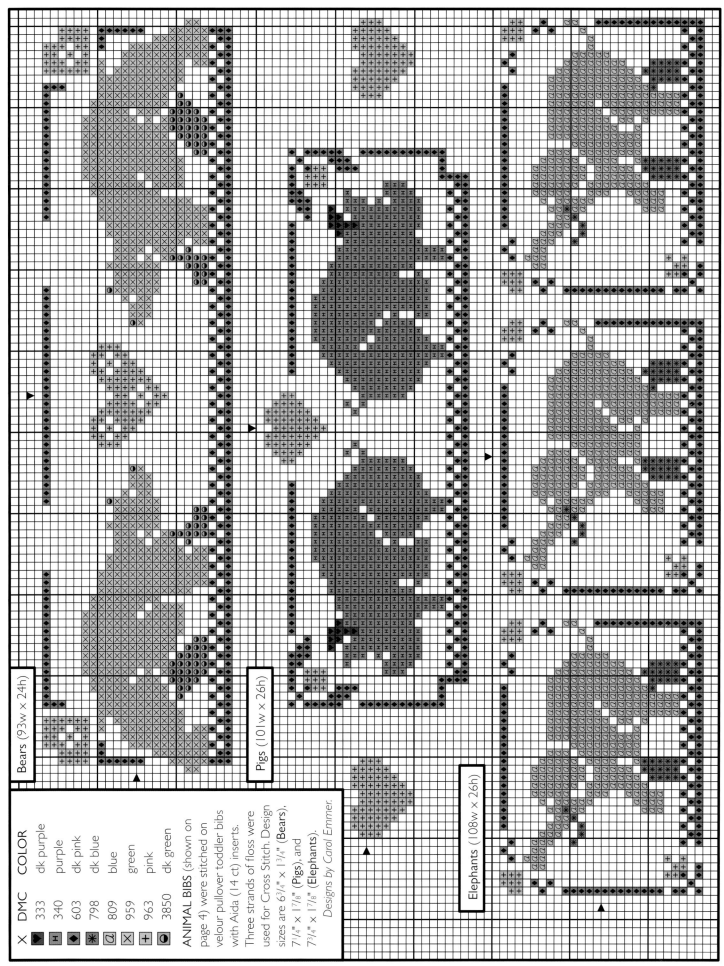

X	DMC	COLOR
◆	333	dk purple
H	340	purple
◆	603	dk pink
✳	798	dk blue
a	809	blue
X	959	green
+	963	pink
◖	3850	dk green

Bears (93w × 24h)

Pigs (101w × 26h)

Elephants (108w × 26h)

ANIMAL BIBS (shown on page 4) were stitched on velour pullover toddler bibs with Aida (14 ct) inserts. Three strands of floss were used for Cross Stitch. Design sizes are 6³/₄" × 1³/₄" (Bears), 7¹/₄" × 1⁷/₈" (Pigs), and 7³/₄" × 1⁷/₈" (Elephants).

Designs by Carol Emmer.

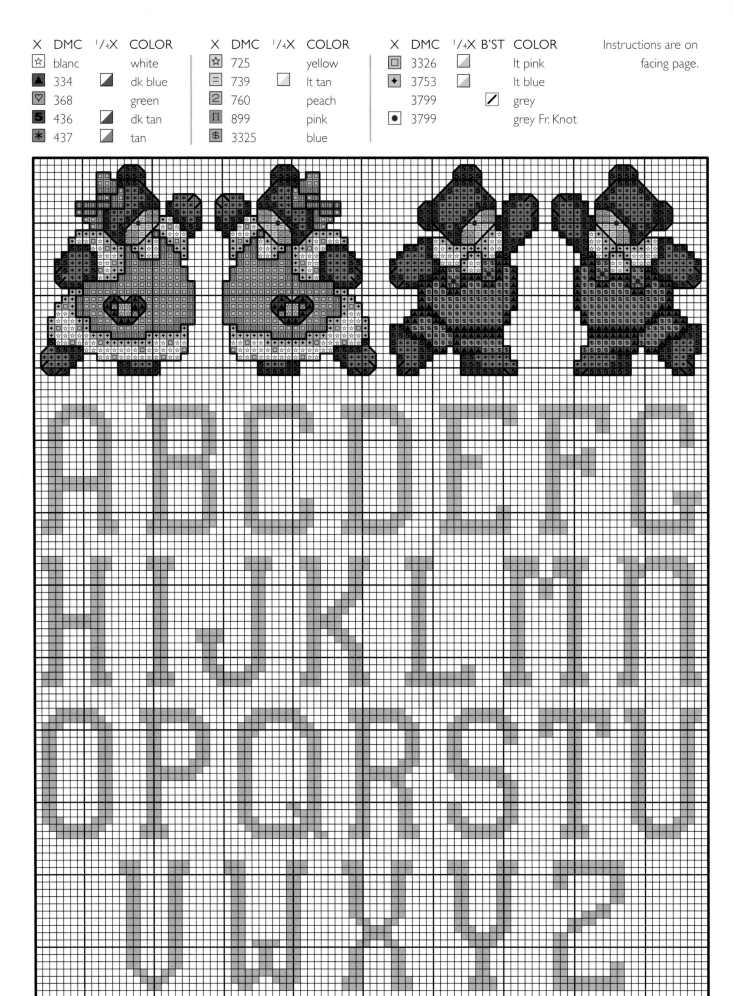

BEARY CUTE BIBS (shown on page 4, chart is on facing page) were stitched on velour pullover toddler bibs with Aida (14 ct) inserts. Three strands of floss were used for Cross Stitch and 1 strand for Backstitch and Fr. Knots. Center and stitch desired name with bottom of letters 3 squares from bottom of insert and leaving 2 squares between letters. Stitch one bear on each end 2 squares from letters. For longer names, count number of squares required to insure adequate space for designs. Use DMC 335 for girl's name and DMC 322 for boy's name.

Designs by Lorri Birmingham.

Baby (93w × 30h)

X	DMC	B'ST	COLOR	X	DMC	COLOR	X	DMC	B'ST	COLOR
•	blanc		white	●	498	dk red	▲	899	/	pink
	310	/	black	$	743	yellow	H	910		green
★	322		blue	Σ	762	grey	d	912		lt green
♥	347		red	✳	775	lt blue	2	3328		lt red
T	437		tan							

BABY TALK (shown on page 5) was stitched on a velour pullover toddler bib with an Aida (14 ct) insert. Two strands of floss were used for Cross Stitch and 1 strand for Backstitch. Design size is 6³/₄"w × 2¹/₄"h.

Design by Patricia Galvan.

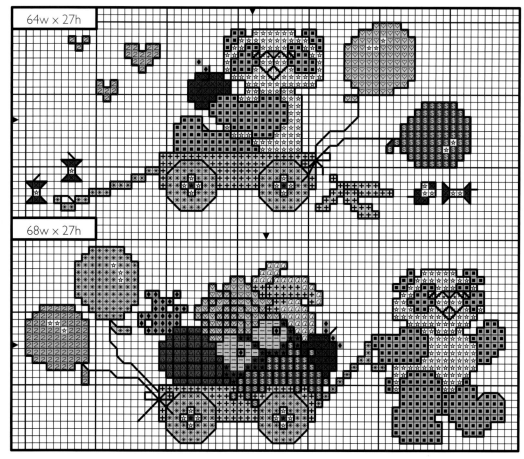

64w × 27h

68w × 27h

X	DMC	¹/₄X	B'ST	COLOR
☆	blanc	◪		white
$	209	◪		purple
✕	309	◪		dk pink
▪	310	◪	/	black
△	437			tan
+	744		☐	dk yellow
a	745			yellow
2	776		◪	pink
◆	913			dk green
♡	955			green
✳	3325		◪	blue
▪	3340			dk peach
—	3341			peach

PANDAS (shown on page 6) were stitched on a velour toddler bib and a velour fingertip towel with Aida (14 ct) inserts. Three strands of floss were used for Cross Stitch and 1 strand for Backstitch. Design sizes are 4⁵/₈"w × 2"h (**Panda in Wagon**) and 4⁷/₈"w × 2"h (**Panda Pulling Wagon**).

Designs by Linda Gillum for Kooler Design Studio.

X	DMC	¼X	B'ST	COLOR
•	blanc			white
▲	340			dk periwinkle
✔	341			periwinkle
⌀	433	◩		brown
₧	435			dk tan
•	436	◪		tan
▢	437	◩		lt tan
⟍	738			vy lt tan
T	744			yellow
•	761			pink
d	762			lt grey
V	813			blue
◑	826			dk blue
4	958		◩	aqua
☆	959			lt aqua
+	964			vy lt aqua
=	3325			lt blue
◉	3340			dk orange
•	3341		◪	orange
8	3371		◩	vy dk brown
✳	3688			mauve
◇	3689			lt mauve
2	3712			dk pink
%	3747			lt periwinkle
5	3812			dk aqua
❖	3822			dk yellow
▼	3824	◩		lt orange
⦿	340			dk periwinkle Fr. Knot
⦿	826			dk blue Fr. Knot
⦿	3371			vy dk brown Fr. Knot

65w × 30h

60w × 31h

60w × 31h

CALICO BIBS (shown on page 7) were stitched on velour pullover toddler bibs with Aida (14 ct) inserts. Three strands of floss were used for Cross Stitch and 1 strand for Backstitch and Fr. Knots. Design sizes are 4³/₄" × 2¹/₄" (Cutie), 4³/₈" × 2¹/₄" (Born in the USA and I'm Hungry as a Bear).

Designs by Lynn Waters Busa.

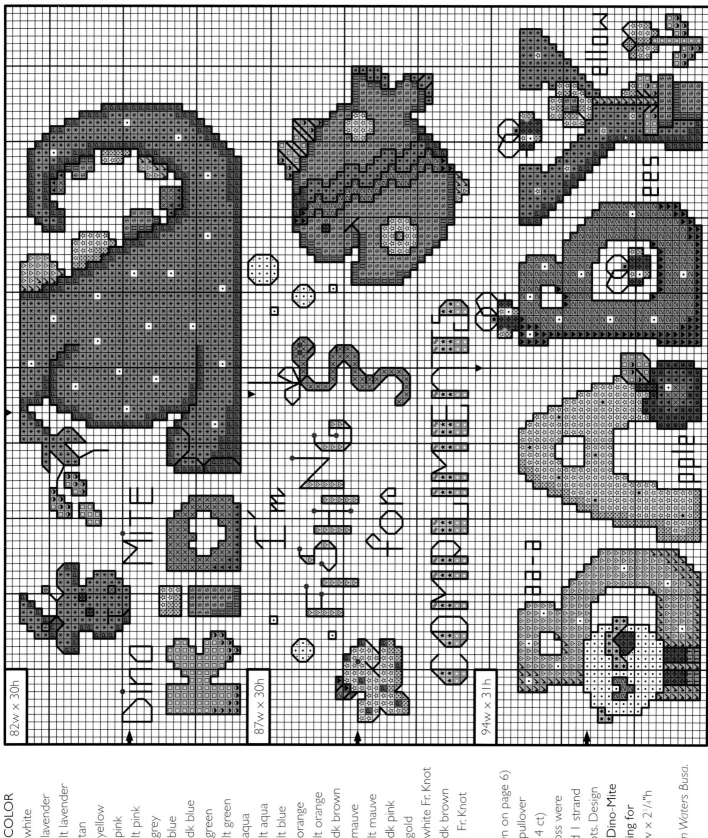

X	DMC	1/4X	B'ST	COLOR
·	blanc			white
P	340			lavender
*	341			lt lavender
T	436			tan
☆	744			yellow
◄	760			pink
✕	761			lt pink
■	762			grey
★	813			blue
◑	826			dk blue
□	912			green
◣	954			lt green
▷	958			aqua
‰	959			lt aqua
∏	3325			lt blue
$	3340			orange
❖	3341			lt orange
►	3371		/	dk brown
2	3688		/	mauve
◊	3689			lt mauve
⁝	3712			dk pink
◦	3822			gold
	blanc			white Fr. Knot
●	3371			dk brown Fr. Knot

DINO-MITE BIBS (shown on page 6) were stitched on velour pullover toddler bibs with Aida (14 ct) inserts. Two strands of floss were used for Cross Stitch and 1 strand for Backstitch and Fr. Knots. Design sizes are 5⅞"w x 2¼"h (Dino-Mite Kid), 6¼"w x 2¼"h (Fishing for Compliments), and 6¾"w x 2¼"h (Baby).

Designs by Lynn Waters Busa.

Design measurements (within chart):
- 82w x 30h
- 87w x 30h
- 94w x 31h

15

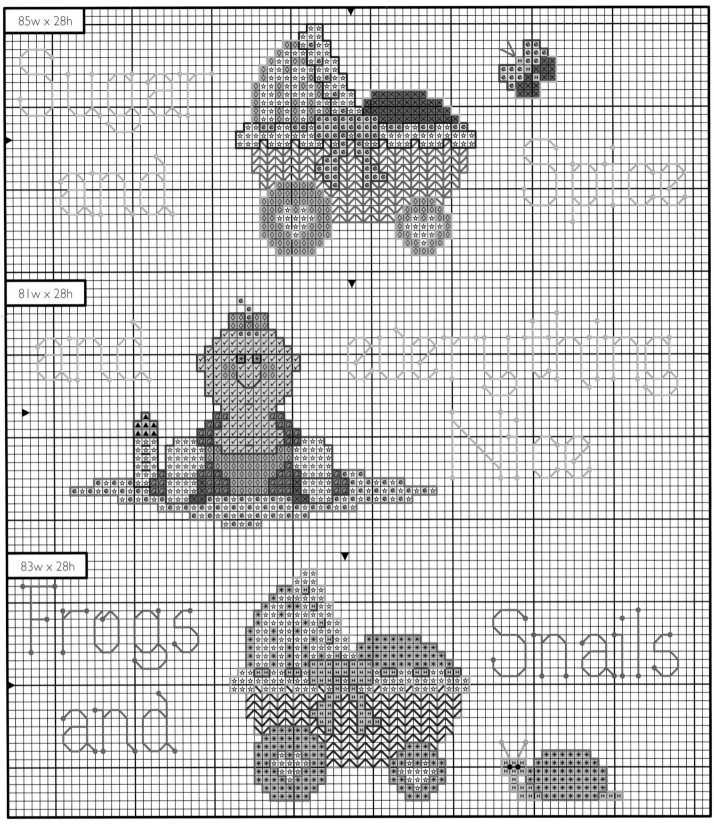

LITTLE GIRLS AND BOYS (shown on page 9) were stitched using 3 strands of floss for Cross Stitch and 1 strand for Backstitch and Fr. Knots. **Sugar and Spice** and **Frogs and Snails** were stitched on velour pullover toddler bibs with Aida (14 ct)

inserts. **Everything Nice** and **Puppy Dogs' Tails** were stitched on velour fingertip towels with Aida (14 ct) inserts. Design sizes are 6¹⁄₈"w × 2"h (**Sugar and Spice**), 5⁷⁄₈"w × 2"h (**Everything Nice**), 6"w × 2"h (**Frogs and Snails**), and 6¹⁄₄"w × 2"h (**Puppy Dog Tails**).

Designs by Terrie Lee Steinmeyer.

CHRISTMAS BIBS (shown on page 8) were stitched on velour pullover toddler bibs with Aida (14 ct) inserts. Three strands of floss were used for Cross Stitch and 1 strand for Backstitch and Fr. Knots. Design sizes are 4¹⁄₂"w × 1³⁄₄"h (**Candy Cane Kid**) and 6"w × 1³⁄₄"h (**Santas**).

Designs by Carol Emmer.

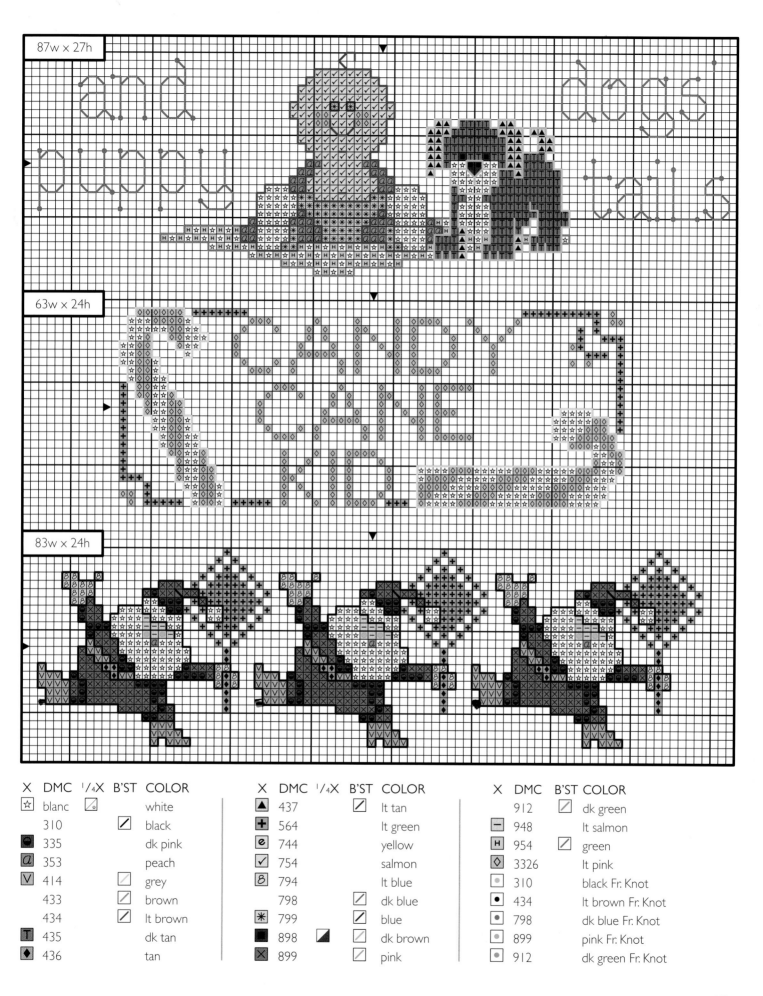

X	DMC	¼X	B'ST	COLOR
☆	blanc	◩		white
	310		⟋	black
◼	335			dk pink
a	353			peach
V	414		⟋	grey
	433		⟋	brown
	434		⟋	lt brown
T	435			dk tan
◆	436			tan

X	DMC	¼X	B'ST	COLOR
▲	437		⟋	lt tan
+	564			lt green
e	744			yellow
✓	754			salmon
8	794			lt blue
	798		⟋	dk blue
✳	799		⟋	blue
◼	898	◪	⟋	dk brown
✕	899			pink

X	DMC	B'ST	COLOR
	912	⟋	dk green
−	948		lt salmon
H	954	⟋	green
◇	3326		lt pink
•	310		black Fr. Knot
●	434		lt brown Fr. Knot
•	798		dk blue Fr. Knot
•	899		pink Fr. Knot
•	912		dk green Fr. Knot

FLORALS

Restful, refreshing blue is a natural backdrop for lovely flowers! Create a Floral Fancy pillow with a multicolor bouquet, a delft-inspired Blue Blossoms pillow and box lid insert, or a cheerful Brown Bagger daisy bouquet to frame.

Charts on are pages 28-30.

The Rosy Bouquet framed piece is extravagantly rich in its array of colors. Like hand-painted tiles, the nine mini-motifs of Spring Finesse are as lovely one-by-one as they are side-by-side. For thoughtful gifts, stitch them to make delicate sachets or a ruffled pillow.

Charts on are pages 32-35.

You can almost smell the spicy scent of violets in Fresh-Picked Bouquets.
Thyme in My Garden celebrates the joys of the herb garden.

Charts on pages 36 and 38-39.

A sprinkling of tiny blooms brightens the border of the Violets Fingertip Towel. A great pick for the needle artist—Floral Needle Cases are pretty ways to help keep a beloved hobby organized. Everyone's favorite old-fashioned annual, Zinnias are meant to be shared from generation to generation, just like this amazing pillow.

Charts on pages 31, 37, and 40-43.

There simply can't be a more charming sight than this ruby-throated fellow as he visits a geranium!
Dance of the Hummingbird is a perfect pillow but would also make a nice framed piece.

Chart is on facing page.

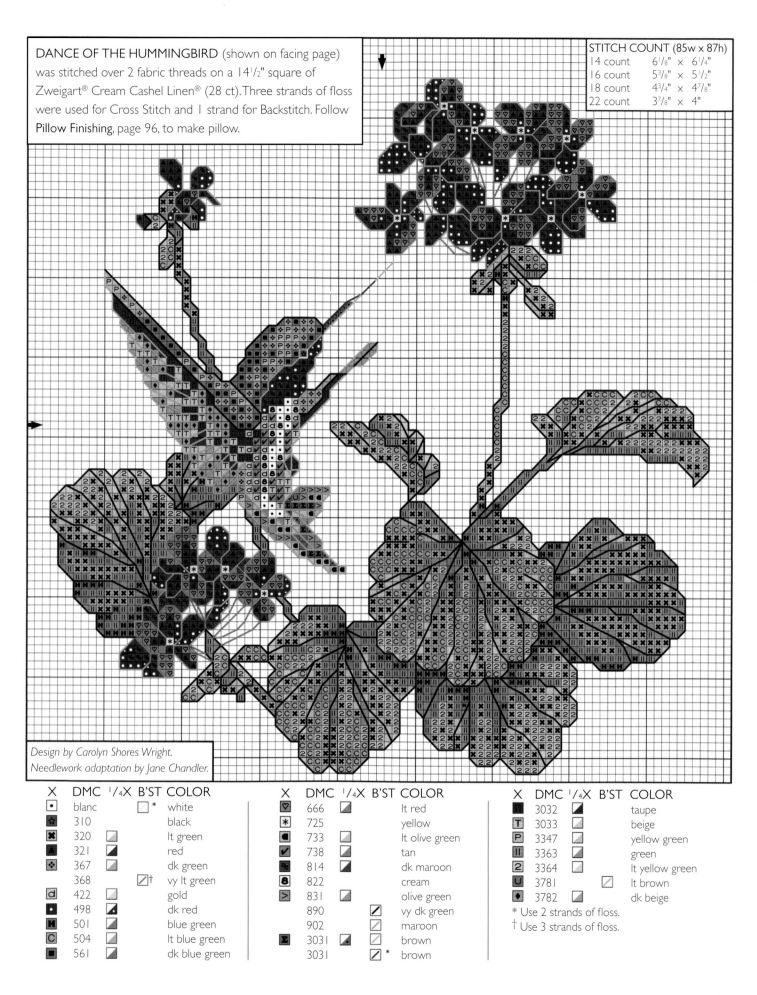

DANCE OF THE HUMMINGBIRD (shown on facing page) was stitched over 2 fabric threads on a 14 1/2" square of Zweigart® Cream Cashel Linen® (28 ct). Three strands of floss were used for Cross Stitch and 1 strand for Backstitch. Follow **Pillow Finishing**, page 96, to make pillow.

Follow **Pillow Finishing**, page 96, to make pillow.

STITCH COUNT (85w x 87h)		
14 count	6 1/8"	x 6 1/4"
16 count	5 3/8"	x 5 1/2"
18 count	4 3/4"	x 4 7/8"
22 count	3 7/8"	x 4"

Design by Carolyn Shores Wright.
Needlework adaptation by Jane Chandler.

X	DMC	1/4X	B'ST	COLOR
•	blanc		*	white
☆	310			black
✖	320	◨		lt green
▲	321	◨		red
❖	367	◨		dk green
	368		◨ †	vy lt green
d	422	◨		gold
●	498	◨		dk red
H	501	◨		blue green
C	504	◨		lt blue green
■	561	◨		dk blue green

X	DMC	1/4X	B'ST	COLOR
♡	666	◨		lt red
✳	725	◨		yellow
◖	733	◨		lt olive green
✓	738	◨		tan
✾	814	◨		dk maroon
8	822	◨		cream
>	831	◨		olive green
	890		◨	vy dk green
	902		◨	maroon
Σ	3031	◨		brown
	3031		◨ *	brown

X	DMC	1/4X	B'ST	COLOR
▤	3032	◨		taupe
T	3033	◨		beige
P	3347	◨		yellow green
‖	3363	◨		green
2	3364	◨		lt yellow green
U	3781		◨	lt brown
◆	3782	◨		dk beige

* Use 2 strands of floss.
† Use 3 strands of floss.

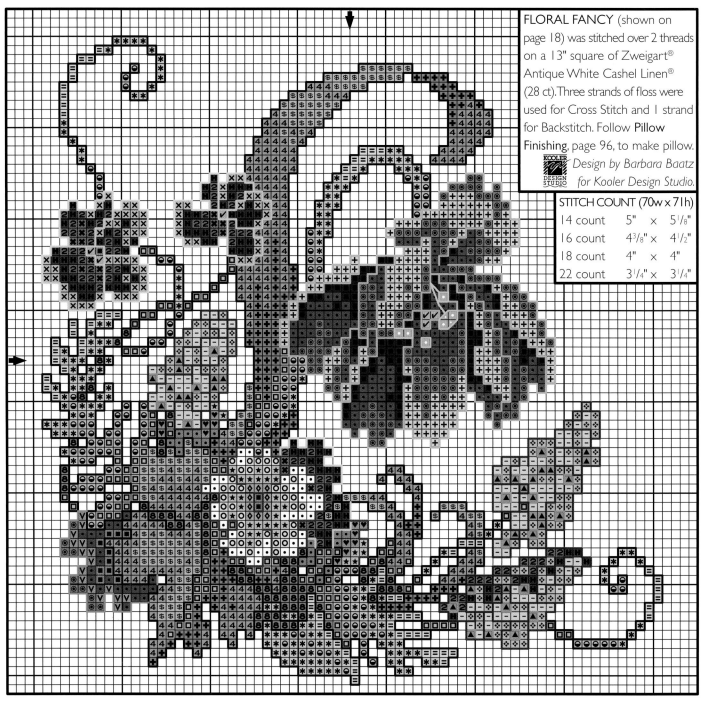

FLORAL FANCY (shown on page 18) was stitched over 2 threads on a 13" square of Zweigart® Antique White Cashel Linen® (28 ct). Three strands of floss were used for Cross Stitch and 1 strand for Backstitch. Follow **Pillow Finishing**, page 96, to make pillow.

Design by Barbara Baatz for Kooler Design Studio.

STITCH COUNT (70w x 71h)

14 count	5" x	5¹/₈"
16 count	4³/₈" x	4¹/₂"
18 count	4" x	4"
22 count	3¹/₄" x	3¹/₄"

X	DMC	¹/₄X	B'ST	COLOR
•	blanc		◩	white
✕	210			vy lt purple
◉	309	◪	◩	lt red
−	341			lt blue
✖	550		◩	dk purple
2	552			purple
V	608 &			orange &
	3340			dk peach
◔	702			dk yellow green
✳	704			yellow green

X	DMC	B'ST	COLOR
★	742		dk yellow
○	745		yellow
=	772		lt yellow green
+	776		pink
▪	781	◩	tan
▲	791	◩	dk blue
■	815	◩	red
8	890	◩	dk green
•	946		dk orange
◎	956		dk pink
♥	971		yellow orange

X	DMC	¹/₄X	B'ST	COLOR
H	3607 &			fuchsia &
	553			lt purple
▫	3799	◪	◩	grey
❖	3807			blue
✚	3815			dk blue green
4	3816			blue green
$	3817			lt blue green
▢	3818			green
◇	3824			peach
✔	3827			lt tan

* Use 2 strands of first color listed and 1 strand of second color listed.

X	DMC	¼X	B'ST	COLOR
▨	791	◪	╱	vy dk blue
V	793			dk blue
◆	794			blue

STITCH COUNT (75w x 75h)

14 count	5³⁄₈"	x	5³⁄₈"
16 count	4³⁄₄"	x	4³⁄₄"
18 count	4¹⁄₄"	x	4¹⁄₄"
22 count	3¹⁄₂"	x	3¹⁄₂"

BLUE BLOSSOMS (shown on page 18) was stitched over 2 fabric threads on a 14" square of Zweigart® Antique White Lugana (25 ct). Three strands of floss were used for Cross Stitch and 1 strand for Backstitch. Design size is 6" x 6". Follow **Pillow Finishing**, page 96, to make pillow.

Box: The center portion of the design was stitched over 2 fabric threads on an 8" square of Zweigart® Antique White Lugana (25 ct). Three strands of floss were used for Cross Stitch and 1 strand for Backstitch. It was inserted in a purchased hinged box with a 5" square opening.

KOOLER DESIGN STUDIO *Design by Kooler Design Studio.*

STITCH COUNT (96w x 140h)
14 count   6⅞" × 10"
16 count   6"   × 8¾"
18 count   5⅜" × 7⅞"
22 count   4⅜" × 6⅜"

Color key and instructions are on facing page.

X	DMC	1/2X	B'ST	COLOR
⊞	blanc			white
	315	▨		mauve
	434		◿	brown
✳	435			vy dk tan
◉	436			dk tan
5	437			tan
−	676			yellow
O	727			lt yellow
V	729			dk yellow
8	738	▢		lt tan
X	739			vy lt tan
	926	▨		dk spruce
✚	927	▨		spruce
◇	928	▢		lt spruce
	931	▨		blue
	932	▢		lt blue
	3032		◿	beige
3	3362	▨		dk green
♦	3363	▨		green
◉	3364			lt green

BROWN BAGGER (shown on page 19, chart is on facing page) was stitched over 2 fabric threads on a 16" × 20" piece of Zweigart® White Lugana (25 ct). Three strands of floss were used for Cross Stitch and 1 strand for Half Cross Stitch and Backstitch. A 14" length of white floss was threaded around the bag and the ends tied in a bow on front. Design size is 7³/₄" × 11¹/₄". Design was custom framed.

Design by Judy Buswell.

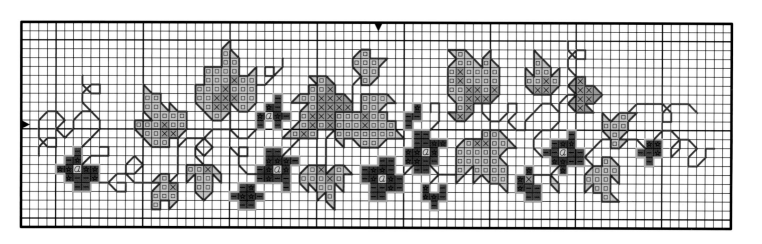

X	DMC	1/4X	B'ST	COLOR
★	208		◿	purple
−	210			lt purple
X	701	◲	◿	green
▢	704	◲		lt green
a	744			yellow

VIOLETS AT YOUR FINGERTIPS (shown on page 24) was stitched on a handtowel with an Aida (14 ct) insert. Three strands of floss were used for Cross Stitch and 1 strand for Backstitch.

*Design by Kooler Design Studio.*

STITCH COUNT (78w × 19h)

14 count	5⁵/₈" × 1³/₈"
16 count	4⁷/₈" × 1¹/₄"
18 count	4³/₈" × 1¹/₈"
22 count	3⁵/₈" × ⁷/₈"

ROSY BOUQUET (shown on page 20) was stitched over
2 fabric threads on a 17" × 21" piece of Zweigart® Antique White
Lugana (25 ct). Three strands of floss were used for Cross Stitch
and 1 strand for Backstitch, unless otherwise indicated in color
key. Design size is 8½" × 12½". Design was custom framed.

Design by Donna Vermillion Giampa.

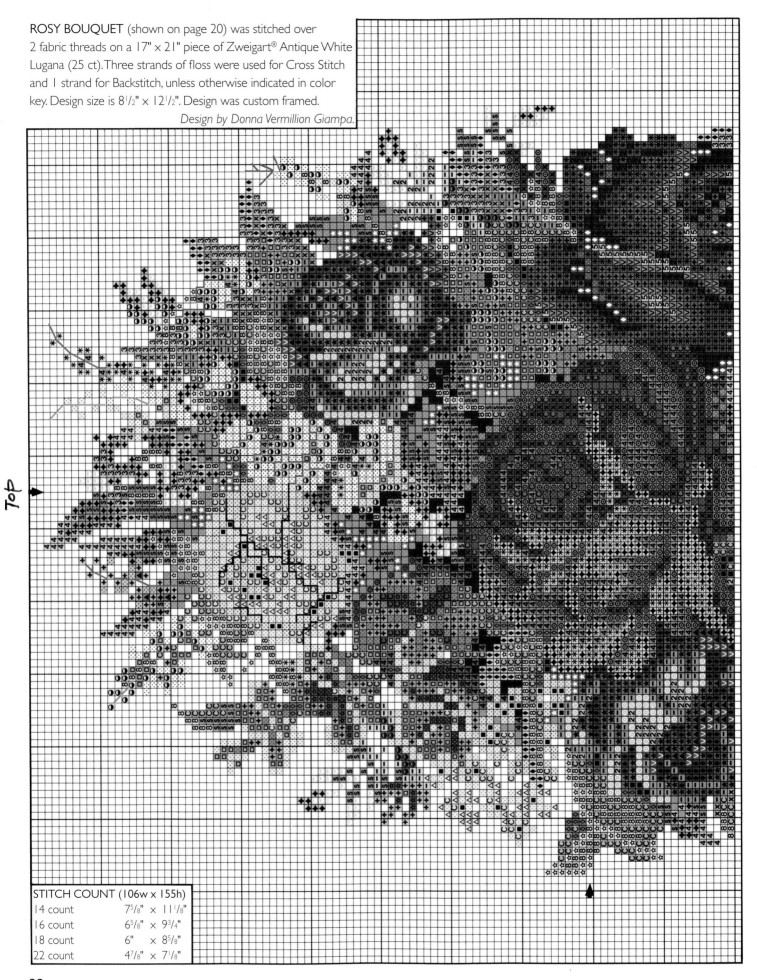

STITCH COUNT (106w x 155h)	
14 count	7⅝" × 11⅛"
16 count	6⅝" × 9¾"
18 count	6" × 8⅝"
22 count	4⅞" × 7⅛"

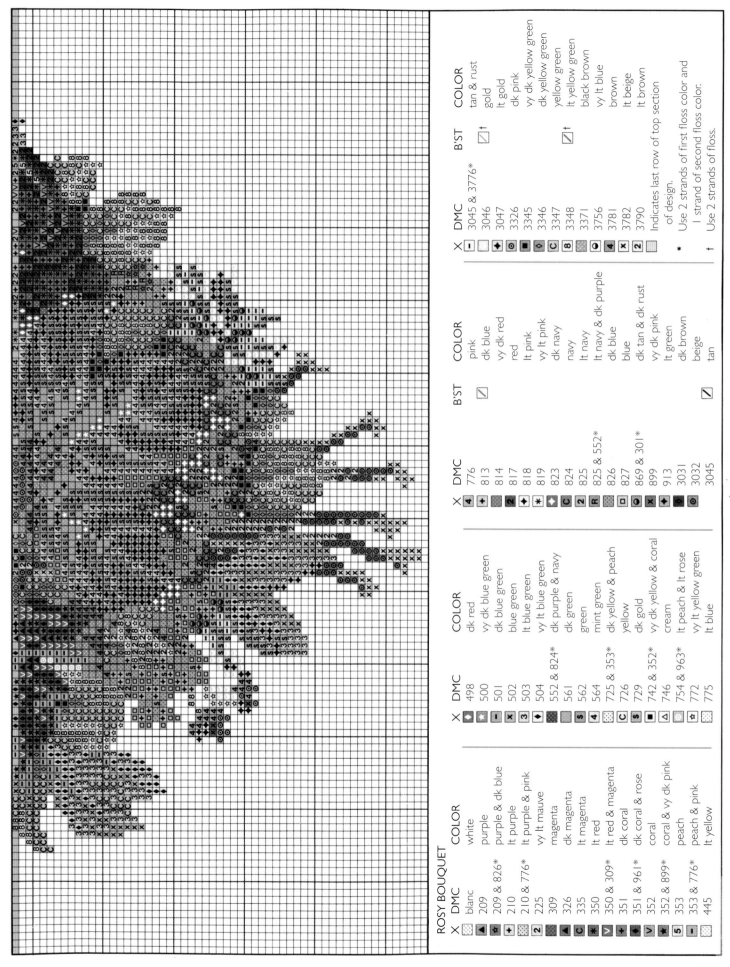

ROSY BOUQUET

X	DMC	COLOR
	blanc	white
	209	purple
	209 & 826*	purple & dk blue
	210	lt purple
	210 & 776*	lt purple & pink
2	225	vy lt mauve
	309	magenta
	326	dk magenta
	335	lt magenta
	350	lt red
C	350 & 309*	lt red & magenta
*	351	dk coral
>	351 & 961*	dk coral & rose
♦	352	coral
V	352 & 899*	coral & vy dk pink
★	353	peach
5	353 & 776*	peach & pink
—	445	lt yellow

X	DMC	COLOR
♦	498	dk red
★	500	vy dk blue green
I	501	dk blue green
×	502	blue green
3	503	lt blue green
♦	504	vy lt blue green
	552 & 824*	dk purple & navy
S	561	dk green
	562	green
4	564	mint green
	725 & 353*	dk yellow & peach
C	726	yellow
S	729	dk gold
■	742 & 352*	vy dk yellow & coral
△	746	cream
⊙	754 & 963*	lt peach & lt rose
☆	772	vy lt yellow green
	775	lt blue

X	DMC	B'ST	COLOR
4	776		pink
+	813		dk blue
	814	◹	vy dk red
2	817		red
♦	818		lt pink
*	819		vy lt pink
◇	823		dk navy
C	824		navy
2	825		lt navy
R	825 & 552*		lt navy & dk purple
	826		dk blue
□	827		blue
⊙	869 & 301*		dk tan & dk rust
×	899		vy dk pink
♦	913		lt green
■	3031		dk brown
⊙	3032		beige
	3045		tan

X	DMC	B'ST	COLOR
I	3045 & 3776*		tan & rust
	3046	◹ †	gold
♦	3047		lt gold
⊙	3326		dk pink
■	3345		vy dk yellow green
◇	3346		dk yellow green
C	3347		yellow green
8	3348		lt yellow green
◐	3371	◹ †	black brown
4	3756		vy lt blue
×	3781		brown
2	3782		lt beige
	3790		lt brown

Indicates last row of top section of design.

* Use 2 strands of first floss color and 1 strand of second floss color.

† Use 2 strands of floss.

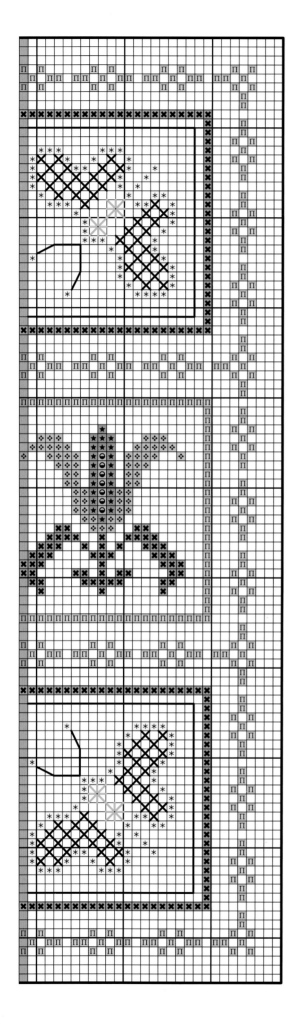

X	DMC	B'ST	COLOR	STITCH COUNT (99w x 99h)	
♥	221		burgundy	14 count	7¹/₈" × 7¹/₈"
▲	223		mauve	16 count	6¹/₄" × 6¹/₄"
$	676		gold	18 count	5¹/₂" × 5¹/₂"
✱	712	╱	cream	22 count	4¹/₂" × 4¹/₂"
◒	729		dk gold		
★	930		dk blue		
❖	931		blue		
✖	3362		dk green		
Π	3363		green		
%	3740		violet		
✳*	712		cream Algerian Eye Stitch		

▨ Indicates last row of left section
of design.

*Use 1 strand of Pearl Cotton #12.

SPRING FINESSE (shown on page 21) was stitched over 2 fabric threads on an 14" square of Zweigart® Putty Cashel Linen® (28 ct). Two strands of floss were used for Cross Stitch and 1 strand for Backstitch unless otherwise noted in the color key. Follow **Pillow Finishing**, page 96, to make pillow.

Sachet Bags: Portions of the design (refer to photo) were stitched over 2 fabric threads on 6" squares of Zweigart® Putty Cashel Linen® (28 ct). Each design was centered horizontally ⁷/₈" above bottom edge of fabric. Two strands of floss were used for Cross Stitch and 1 strand for Backstitch unless otherwise noted in the color key.

For each sachet bag, you will need an 18" length of ¹/₄"w ribbon, polyester fiberfill, and scented oil.

Note: Use ¹/₂" seam allowance for all seams.

Matching right sides and side raw edges, fold linen square in half. Sew sides together and press seam allowances open. With seam at center back, sew across bottom of bag. Trim seam allowances diagonally at corners. Turn sachet bag right side out, carefully pushing corners outward. Turn top edge ¹/₂" to wrong side and press; turn ¹/₂" to wrong side again and hem. Stuff bag with polyester fiberfill. Place a few drops of scented oil on a small amount of fiberfill and insert in center of stuffed bag so that oil doesn't touch linen. Tie ribbon in a bow around bag; trim ends as desired.

Design by Anne Stanton.

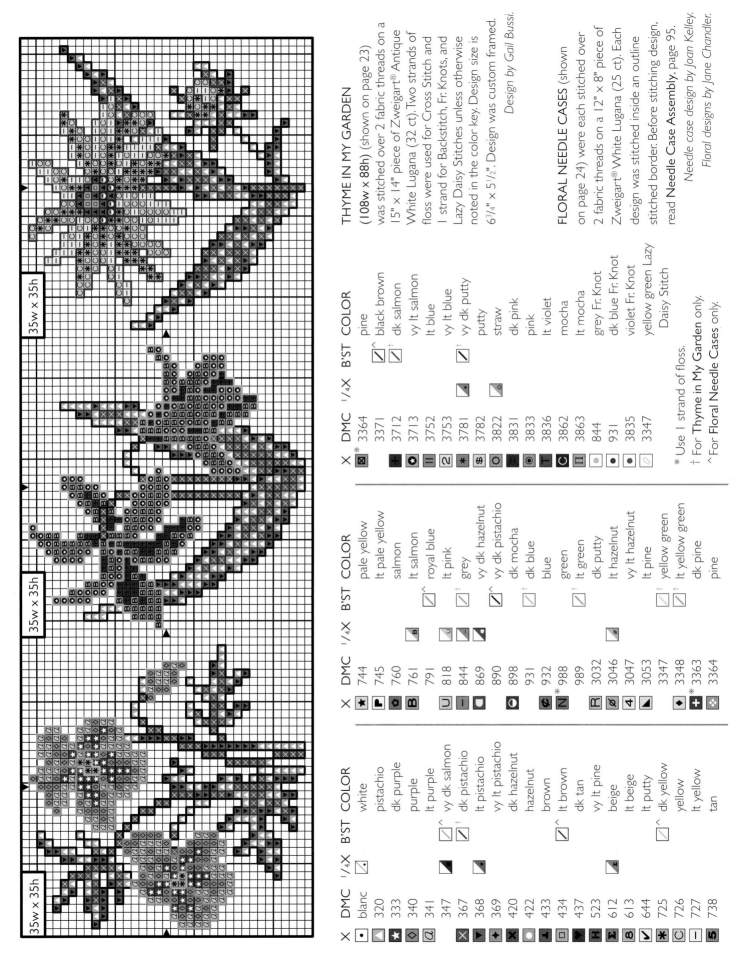

35w x 35h · 35w x 35h · 35w x 35h · 35w x 35h

THYME IN MY GARDEN

(108w x 88h) (shown on page 23) was stitched over 2 fabric threads on a 15" x 14" piece of Zweigart® Antique White Lugana (32 ct). Two strands of floss were used for Cross Stitch and 1 strand for Backstitch, Fr. Knots, and Lazy Daisy Stitches unless otherwise noted in the color key. Design size is 6¾" x 5½". Design was custom framed.

Design by Gail Bussi.

FLORAL NEEDLE CASES

(shown on page 24) were each stitched over 2 fabric threads on a 12" x 8" piece of Zweigart® White Lugana (25 ct). Each design was stitched inside an outline stitched border. Before stitching design, read Needle Case Assembly, page 95.

Needle case design by Joan Kelley.
Floral designs by Jane Chandler.

X	DMC	1/4X	B'ST	COLOR
	blanc	⊡		white
	320			pistachio
	333			dk purple
	340			purple
	341			lt purple
	347		^	vy dk salmon
	367		†	dk pistachio
	368			lt pistachio
	369			vy lt pistachio
	420			dk hazelnut
	422			hazelnut
	433			brown
	434		^	lt brown
	437			dk tan
	523			vy lt pine
	612			beige
	613			lt beige
	644			lt putty
	725		^	dk yellow
	726			yellow
	727			lt yellow
	738			tan

X	DMC	1/4X	B'ST	COLOR
	744			pale yellow
	745			lt pale yellow
	760			salmon
	761		^	lt salmon
	791			royal blue
	818			lt pink
	844		†	grey
	869			vy dk hazelnut
	890		^	vy dk pistachio
	898			dk mocha
	931			dk blue
	932		†	blue
*	988			green
	989		†	lt green
	3032			dk putty
	3046			lt hazelnut
	3047			vy lt hazelnut
	3053			lt pine
	3347			yellow green
	3348		†	lt yellow green
*	3363		†	dk pine
	3364			pine

X	DMC	1/4X	B'ST	COLOR
*	3364			pine
	3371		^	black brown
	3712		^	dk salmon
	3713			vy lt salmon
	3752			lt blue
	3753			vy lt blue
	3781		^	vy dk putty
	3782			putty
	3822			straw
	3831			dk pink
	3833			pink
	3836			lt violet
	3862	*		mocha
	3863			lt mocha
	844	o		grey Fr. Knot
	931			dk blue Fr. Knot
	3835			violet Fr. Knot
	3347			yellow green Lazy Daisy Stitch

* Use 1 strand of floss.
† For Thyme in My Garden only.
^ For Floral Needle Cases only.

X	DMC	B'ST	COLOR	X	DMC	COLOR	STITCH COUNT
☆	blanc		white	⊟	987	green	(61w x 82h)
■	349		red	5	989	lt green	14 count 4³/₈" x 5⁷/₈"
+	726		yellow	Ⅱ	3839	lavender	16 count 3⁷/₈" x 5¹/₈"
	938	╱	dk brown	♥	3840	lt lavender	18 count 3¹/₂" x 4⁵/₈"
◉	964		lt teal	e	3848	teal	22 count 2⁷/₈" x 3³/₄"

FORGET ME NOT and WOOD VIOLETS (shown on page 22) were each stitched over 2 fabric threads on a 13" x 15" piece of Zweigart® Antique White Lugana (25 ct). Three strands of floss were used for Cross Stitch and 1 strand for Backstitch and Fr. Knots. Design sizes are 5" x 6⁵/₈" (Forget me Not) and 5¹/₈" x 6⁵/₈" (Wood Violets). Designs were custom framed.

Designs by Polly Carbonari.

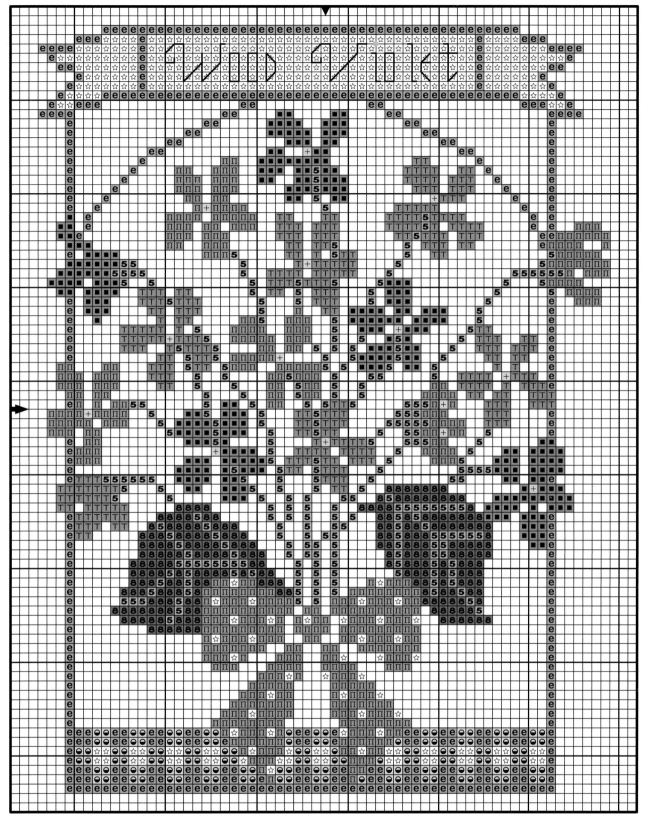

X	DMC	B'ST	COLOR		X	DMC	COLOR	STITCH COUNT
☆	blanc		white		◖	964	lt teal	(63w x 82h)
Π	316		lt mauve		8	987	green	14 count 4½" x 5⅞"
T	553		lt purple		5	989	lt green	16 count 4" x 5⅛"
+	726		yellow		e	3848	teal	18 count 3½" x 4⅝"
■	793		blue		●	938	dk brown	22 count 2⅞" x 3¾"
	938	╱	dk brown				Fr. Knot	

STITCH COUNT (108w x 125h)

14 count	7³/₄" x 9"
16 count	6³/₄" x 7⁷/₈"
18 count	6" x 7"
22 count	5" x 5³/₄"

ZINNIAS (shown on page 25, chart is on pages 40-43) was stitched over 2 fabric threads on a 14" x 15" piece of Zweigart® Mint Green Cashel Linen® (28 ct). Three strands of floss were used for Cross Stitch and 1 strand for Backstitch unless otherwise noted in key. Design size is 7³/₄" x 9". See Pillow Finishing, page 96, to make pillow.

Design by Paula Vaughan.

X	DMC	B'ST	COLOR
I	153		lt lavender
⊕	223		shell pink
▢	316		mauve
#	320		pistachio
◤	327		vy dk purple
◈	349		dk red
5	350	⌐red	red
∨	921		lt rust
◁	351	⌐*	lt red
<	740		dk orange
+	352		vy lt red
◀	355	†★	brick
S	367		dk pistachio
T	369	+	lt pistachio
C	433		brown
2	471		lime
¢	472		lt lime
¢	524		lt avocado
¥	552	⌐*	dk purple
Y	553		purple
)	209		dk lavender
Ⓝ	554	Ⓝ*	lt purple
✳	210		lavender
II	605		pink
⌐	726	⌐*	yellow
✳	3821		lt gold
II	727		lt yellow
⊕	742		lt orange
L	746		cream
O	760	⌐*	lt coral
←	352		vy lt red
1	776		lt rose
◆	781		dk gold
	832	⌐†	golden olive
	833		lt golden olive
	917		dk fuchsia
	918		dk rust

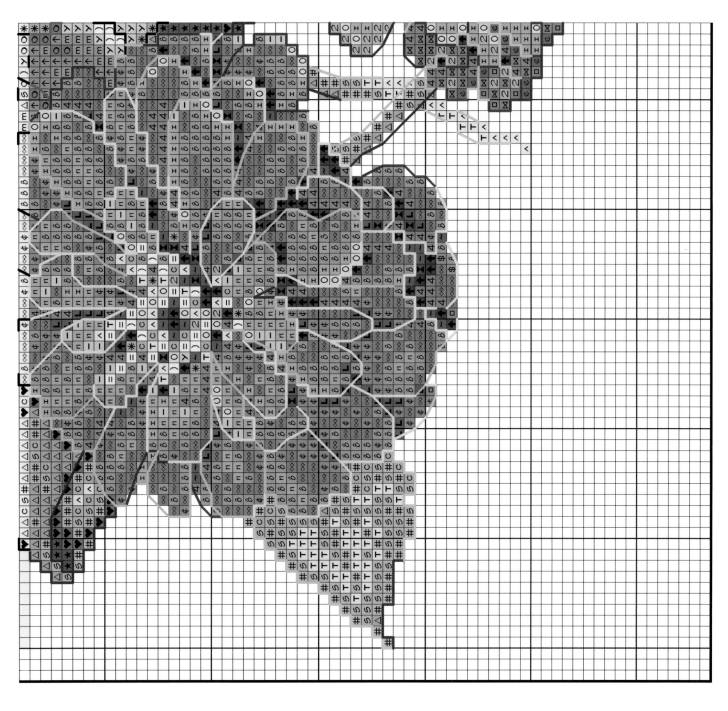

⊠	920	+ rust
★	934	° dk avocado
∂	938	dk brown
○	963	vy lt rose
◆	3041	° antique violet
←	3350	★ raspberry
▶	3362	avocado
8	3607	fuchsia
▶	3608	lt fuchsia
4	3685	dk plum
	3687	plum
⊡	3687	plum
	3350	*[raspberry
⊠	3688	lt plum
	316	*[mauve
∪	3705	coral
	3832	*[dk rose
2	3727	lt mauve
▷	3803	dk mauve
8	3806	dk pink
	3820	gold
ᵐ	833	*[lt golden olive
	3833	rose
∩	351	*[lt red
	3853	vy lt rust
H	741	*[orange
▢		Indicates last row of previous section of design.

* Use 2 strands of the first floss color listed and 1 of the second.

† DMC 355 for orange and coral flower petals. DMC 781 for yellow flower petals.

★ DMC 367 for leaves and stems. DMC 3350 for pink flower petals.

+ DMC 433 for yellow flower petals. DMC 920 for coral flower petals.

° DMC 934 for leaves and stems. DMC 3041 for pink flower petals and signature.

41

Chart continued from page 41.

X	DMC	B'ST	COLOR
I	153		lt lavender
6§	223		shell pink
□	316		mauve
#	320		pistachio
◧	327	/	vy dk purple
◇	349		dk red
5	350		red *lt rust
	921		
Y	351	/ †	lt red *dk orange
	740		
+	352		vy lt red
◣	355	/ ★	brick
◁	367	/	dk pistachio
<	369		lt pistachio
✛	433	/	brown
S	471		lime
T	472		lt lime
C	524		lt avocado
◪	552		dk purple
⊄	553		purple *dk lavender
	209		
⊐	554		lt purple *lavender
	210		
I	605		pink
Y	726		yellow *lt gold
	3821		
)	727		lt yellow
✳	742		lt orange
=	746		cream
⊕	760		lt coral *vy lt red
	352		
L	776		lt rose
O	781	/ †	dk gold
←	832		golden olive *lt golden olive
	833		
◼	917		dk fuchsia
◆	918		dk rust

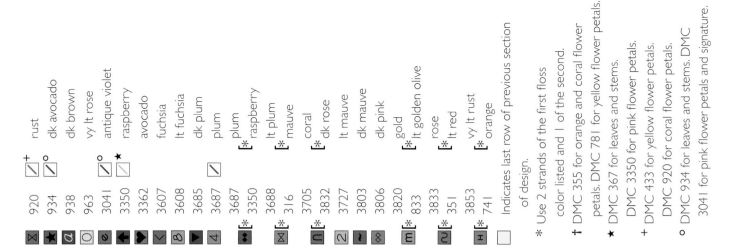

☒	⊞+	920	rust
★	⊘	934	dk avocado
ⓐ	⊘	938	dk brown
○		963	vy lt rose
⊘	⊘°	3041	antique violet
◀	⊘	3350	raspberry
▶		3362	avocado
∨		3607	fuchsia
᠑		3608	lt fuchsia
▶		3685	dk plum
4	⊘	3687	plum
⧎	*[	3687	plum
		3350	raspberry
☒	*[	3688	lt plum
		316	mauve
∪	*[	3705	coral
2		3832	dk rose
⌇		3727	lt mauve
⊗		3803	dk mauve
⧉	*[	3806	dk pink
		3820	gold
☒	*[	833	lt golden olive
		3833	rose
∪	*[	351	lt red
		3853	vy lt rust
H	*[	741	orange
☐			Indicates last row of previous section of design.

* Use 2 strands of the first floss color listed and 1 of the second.
† DMC 355 for orange and coral flower petals. DMC 781 for yellow flower petals.
★ DMC 367 for leaves and stems.
  DMC 3350 for pink flower petals.
+ DMC 433 for yellow flower petals.
  DMC 920 for coral flower petals.
○ DMC 934 for leaves and stems. DMC 3041 for pink flower petals and signature.

The entreaty to Bless Our Home is beautifully stitched with angels watching over a cottage in a flower garden. If you know a quilter, she (or he) would enjoy the patchwork motifs of Blessed are the Piecemakers.

Charts are on pages 55-57.

A sampling of samplers—the small designs on this page are quick to stitch for last-minute gifts. And there are times when it's good to remember the value of Pleasant Words.

Charts are on pages 57-59.

School Days and Noah's Ark samplers are a tribute to the era when children learned to stitch while making simple designs like these. The Gift Samplers are lovely ways to celebrate a birthday or extend your gratitude to someone who's been truly thoughtful.

Charts are on pages 60-61 and 63.

What are the things for which you are grateful? Here are ways to Give Thanks and celebrate living in a nation where Old Glory waves freely. The Hearts and Flowers Sampler is a rustic homage to our stitchery heritage.

Charts are on pages 62 and 64-66.

Through the decades, stitchers have enjoyed portraying the quiet Peace of the world in winter. Another fond theme is honoring the Thanksgiving tradition as a day of gratitude for Peace and Plenty.

Charts are on pages 67-69.

Angels Unawares is a sweet reminder to believers that even a stranger may turn out to be a truer friend than they can guess.

Chart is on pages 70-71.

X	DMC	COLOR	X	DMC	COLOR	X	DMC	COLOR
★	913	green	⬙	754	peach	↘	309	dk pink
T	3761	blue	✕	783	dk yellow	■	310	black
▨		Indicates last row of top section of design.	◁	799	dk blue	✳	415	grey
			⊞	840	brown	☑	472	lt green
			◀	899	pink	⊕	743	yellow

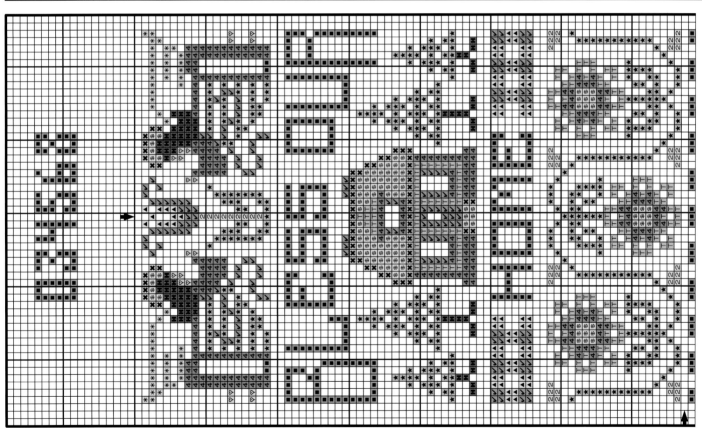

STITCH COUNT (51w x 153h)

14 count	3³/₄" x 11"
16 count	3¹/₄" x 9⁵/₈"
18 count	2⁷/₈" x 8¹/₂"
22 count	2³/₈" x 7"

BLESS OUR HOME (shown on page 44) was stitched on a 12" × 20" piece of Antique White Aida (14 ct). Three strands of floss were used for Cross Stitch. Personalize year with numerals provided. Design was custom framed.

Design by Deborah A. Lambein.

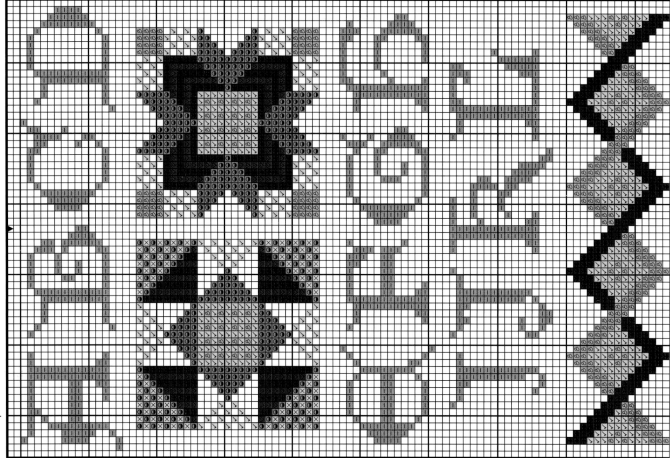

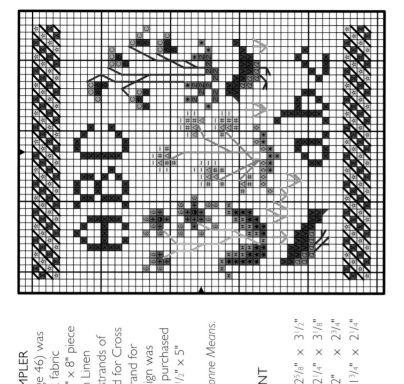

GARDEN SAMPLER

(shown on page 46) was stitched over 2 fabric threads on a 7" × 8" piece of Natural Irish Linen (28 ct). Three strands of floss were used for Cross Stitch and 1 strand for Backstitch. Design was inserted into a purchased frame with a 3½" × 5" opening.

Design by Yvonne Means.

STITCH COUNT (36w x 49h)

14 count	2⅝"	×	3½"
16 count	2¼"	×	3⅛"
18 count	2"	×	2¾"
22 count	1¾"	×	2¼"

X	²	DMC	³/₄X	B'ST	COLOR
2		936		/	dk green
		937		/	green
		938	◨	/	brown
◐		3021			grey
⊠		3371			dk brown
+		3687			dk pink
6		3688			pink
C		3746			lt purple
✕		Brown Kreinik #8 Braid - 022 Antique			
		Copper Kreinik Cord - 215c			

X		DMC	B'ST	COLOR
☆		ecru		ecru
▶		300		rust
a		301		lt rust
8		333		purple
✳		469	/	lt green
◇		470		vy lt green
★		500	/	dk blue green
H		501		blue green
△		742		dk yellow
#		743		yellow
I		744		lt yellow

Bottom Section

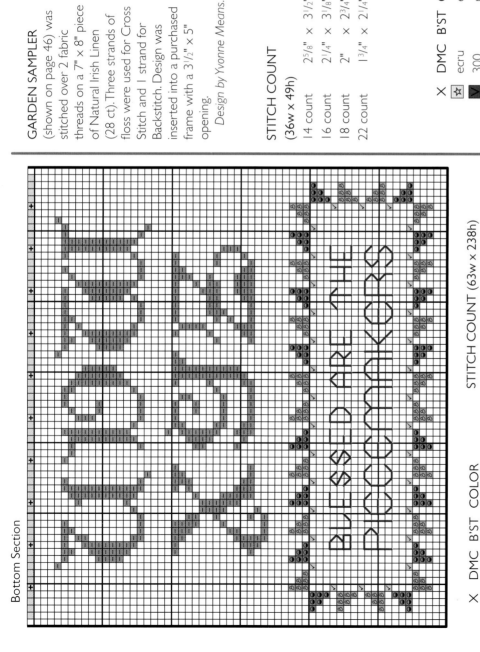

STITCH COUNT (63w x 238h)

14 count	4½"	×	17"
16 count	4"	×	14⅞"
18 count	3½"	×	13¼"
22 count	2⅞"	×	10⅞"

BLESSED ARE THE PIECEMAKERS

(shown on page 45) was stitched over 2 fabric threads on an 11" × 23" piece of Natural Irish Linen (28 ct). Three strands of floss were used for Cross Stitch and 2 strands for Backstitch. Design was custom framed.

Design by Maryanne Moreck.

X		DMC	B'ST	COLOR
▶		304		lt red
■		814		red
⊠		931		lt blue
⋗		3045		gold
8		3051		green
◐		3750	/	blue
I		3790		brown
▨				Indicates last row of top section of design.
▨				Indicates last row of middle section of design.

STITCH COUNTS: 1. (40w x 51h) 2. (39w x 59h) 3. (43w x 49h)
OLD-TIME MINI SAMPLERS (shown on page 46) were each stitched over 2 fabric threads on a 8" x 9" piece of Tea-Dyed Irish Linen (28 ct). Three strands of floss were used for Cross Stitch and Satin Stitch (page 94), and 1 strand for Backstitch. For dates and initials, use DMC 931 for design 1 and DMC 924 for designs 2 and 3. The designs were inserted in purchased frames with 4" x 5" openings. Design sizes are 1. 2⅞" x 3¾", 2. 2⅞" x 4¼", and 3. 3⅛" x 3½".

Designs by Deborah Payne Baker.

X	DMC	B'ST	COLOR	X	DMC	SATIN STITCH	B'ST	COLOR
⬮	315	╱	mauve					
◇	316		lt mauve	⊥	924		╱	blue
☆	680	╱	gold	ⓐ	926	╱		lt blue
−	761		rose	✳	3051		╱	green

PLEASANT WORDS SAMPLER (shown on page 47) was stitched over 2 fabric threads on a 15" × 16" piece of Zweigart® Raw Cashel Linen® (28 ct). Three strands of floss were used for Cross Stitch and 1 strand for Backstitch and Fr. Knots. Design was custom framed.

Design by Charlotte Holder.

X	DMC	B'ST	COLOR
✳	221		dk pink
T	223		pink
V	676		lt gold
◆	729		gold
◥	746	✓	cream
■	930		dk blue
%	932		blue

X	DMC	B'ST	COLOR
◤	3051	✓	dk green
π	3053		green
◉	3371		brown
2	3753		lt blue
◩	3829		dk gold
•	3051		dk green Fr. Knot

STITCH COUNT (92w × 105h)

14 count	6⅝"	× 7½"
16 count	5¾"	× 6⅝"
18 count	5⅛"	× 5⅞"
22 count	4¼"	× 4⅞"

59

X	DMC	B'ST	COLOR
■	315		mauve
■	844	◪	charcoal
★	931		blue
✚	3362		green
✔	3790		khaki
▨	Indicates last row of left section of design.		

STITCH COUNT (109w x 87h)

14 count	$7^{7}/_{8}$"	x $6^{1}/_{4}$"
16 count	$6^{7}/_{8}$"	x $5^{1}/_{2}$"
18 count	$6^{1}/_{8}$"	x $4^{7}/_{8}$"
22 count	5"	x 4"

NOAH'S ARK (shown on page 48) was stitched over 2 fabric threads on a 16" x 14" piece of Zweigart® Platinum Cashel Linen® (28 ct). Three strands of floss were used for Cross Stitch and 1 strand for Backstitch. Design was custom framed.

Design by Kandace Thomas.

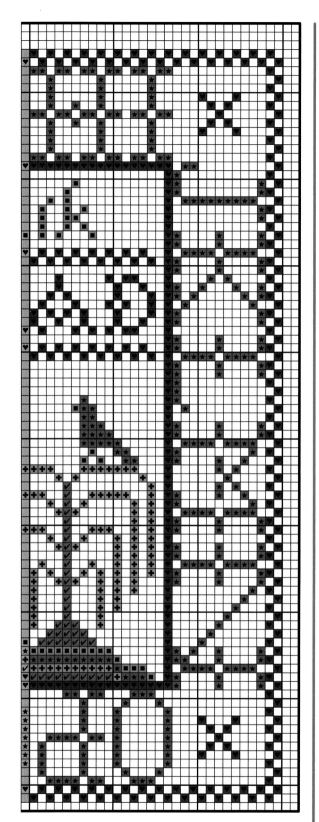

X	DMC	1/4X	B'ST	COLOR	STITCH COUNT (43w x 70h)		
•	blanc		*	white	14 count	3¹/₈"	x 5"
■	310			black	16 count	2³/₄"	x 4³/₈"
◖	414			grey	18 count	2¹/₂"	x 4"
✖	553			purple	22 count	2"	x 3¹/₄"
▼	666			red			
H	700			green	**SCHOOL DAYS** (shown on page 48)
T	738			tan	was stitched over 2 fabric threads on
$	743			yellow	an 11" x 14" piece of Antique White
✔	801			brown	Lugana (25 ct). Two strands of floss
★	825			blue	were used for Cross Stitch and
	938			dk brown	1 strand for Backstitch and Fr. Knots,
▲	3716			pink	unless otherwise noted. Design size is
●	666			red	3¹/₂" x 5⁵/₈". Design was custom framed.
			Fr. Knot		*Design by Polly Carbonari.*

*Use 2 strands of floss.

X	DMC	COLOR
+	336	blue
■	815	red

STITCH COUNT
(59w x 99h)

14 count	4¼" × 7⅛"
16 count	3¾" × 6¼"
18 count	3⅜" × 5½"
22 count	2¾" × 4½"

HEARTS & FLOWERS SAMPLER (shown on page 51) was stitched over 2 fabric threads on a 13" × 16" piece of Cream Irish Linen (28 ct). Two strands of floss were used for Cross Stitch. Design was custom framed.

Design by Leta Sullins.

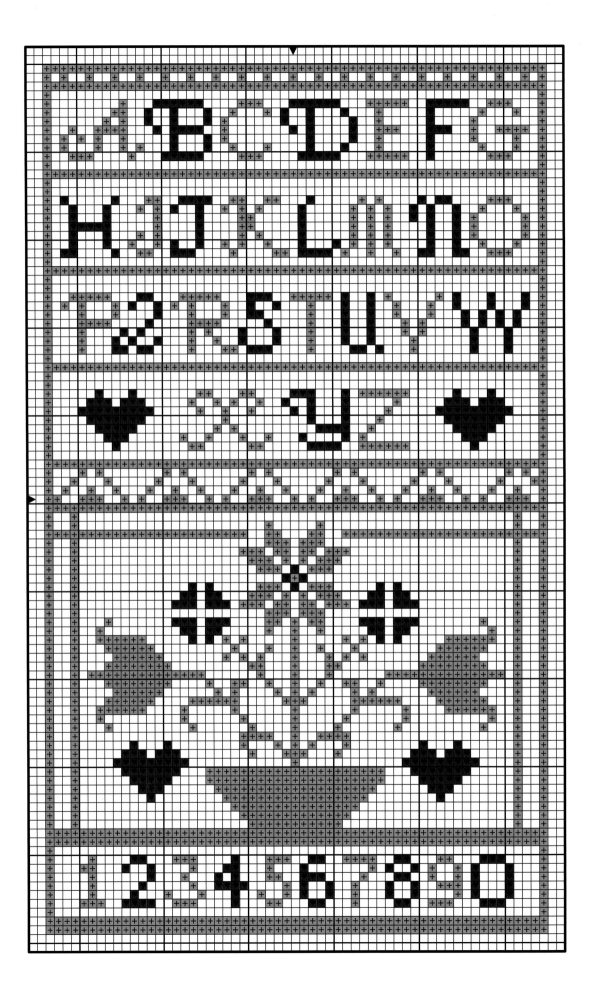

X	DMC	1/4X	B'ST	COLOR
☆	blanc		◫	white
◧	208			dk purple
✚	209			purple
◇	210			lt purple
◀	322			dk blue
✳	562			dk green
◐	563			green
I	743			yellow
◁	3325			blue
▶	3326			rose
◫	3688			pink
⊠	3689			lt pink
	3799		◿	grey
●	3799			grey Fr. Knot

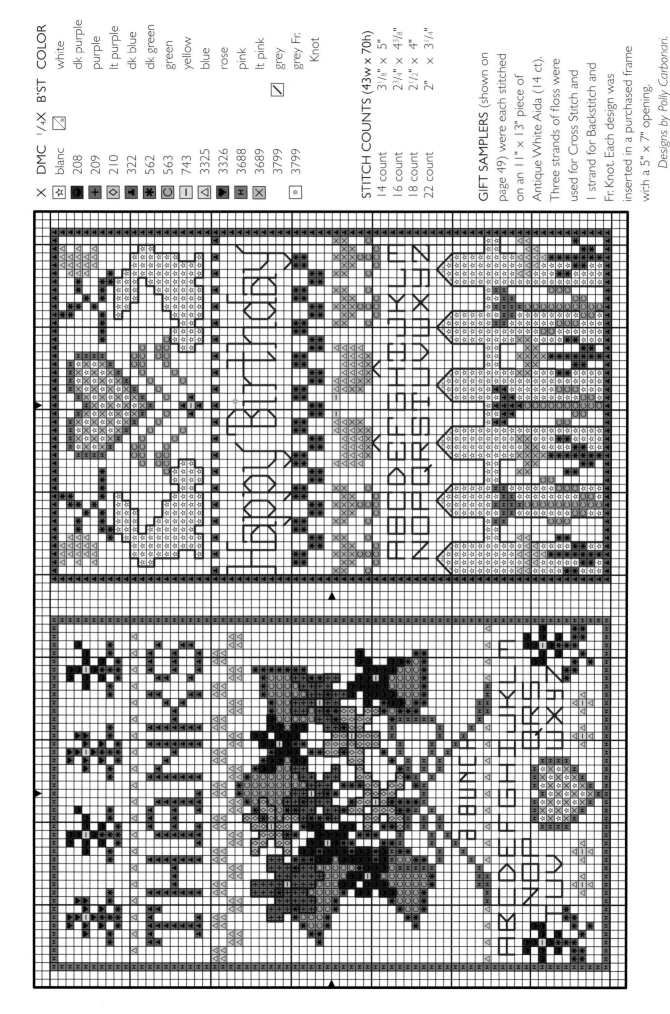

STITCH COUNTS (43w x 70h)

14 count	3 1/8"	x 5"
16 count	2 3/4"	x 4 3/8"
18 count	2 1/2"	x 4"
22 count	2"	x 3 1/4"

GIFT SAMPLERS (shown on page 49) were each stitched on an 11" x 13" piece of Antique White Aida (14 ct). Three strands of floss were used for Cross Stitch and 1 strand for Backstitch and Fr. Knot. Each design was inserted in a purchased frame with a 5" x 7" opening.

Designs by Polly Carbonari.

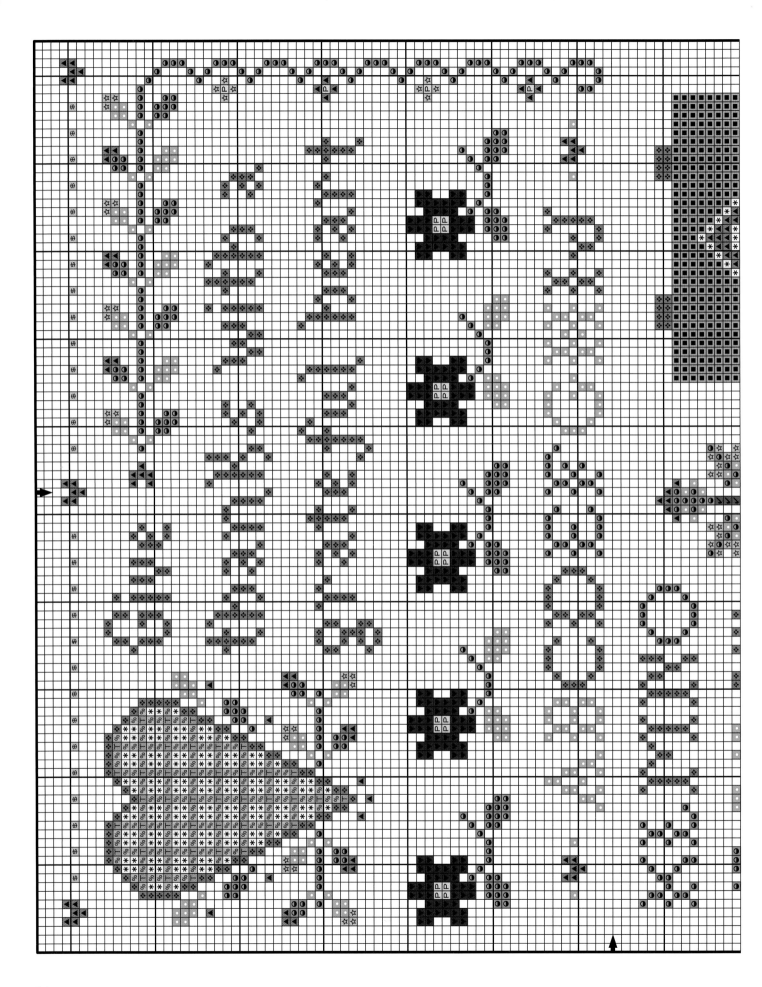

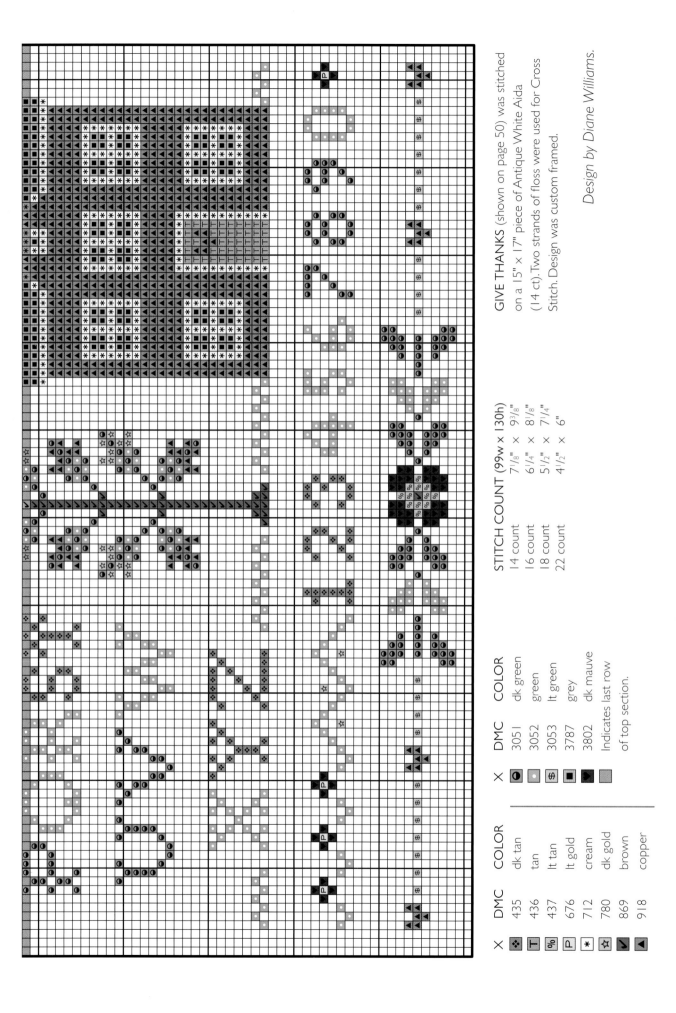

GIVE THANKS (shown on page 50) was stitched on a 15" × 17" piece of Antique White Aida (14 ct). Two strands of floss were used for Cross Stitch. Design was custom framed.

Design by Diane Williams.

STITCH COUNT (99w x 130h)

14 count	7 1/8"	×	9 3/8"
16 count	6 1/4"	×	8 1/8"
18 count	5 1/2"	×	7 1/4"
22 count	4 1/2"	×	6"

X	DMC	COLOR
◐	3051	dk green
⦁	3052	green
$	3053	lt green
■	3787	grey
▶	3802	dk mauve
▦		Indicates last row of top section.

X	DMC	COLOR
❖	435	dk tan
T	436	tan
%	437	lt tan
P	676	lt gold
*	712	cream
☆	780	dk gold
◣	869	brown
◀	918	copper

65

OLD GLORY (shown on page 51) was stitched over 2 fabric threads on a 13" x 14" piece of Shell Linen (28 ct) using a combination of Sampler Threads by The Gentle Art and DMC floss. (If you prefer to use DMC floss only, DMC floss substitute colors are provided.) Two strands of floss or Sampler Threads were used for Cross Stitch and 1 strand for Backstitch. A small star charm was attached using 1 strand of DMC 729 floss. Design was custom framed.

Design by Kathy Elrod.

X	SAMPLER THREAD	DMC	¼X	¾X	B'ST	COLOR
8	Raspberry Parfait	221	◩		◪	dk mauve
✔		610				dk khaki
•	Flax	612	◪			khaki
5	Gold Leaf	729	◪			gold
◣		780	◩		◪	dk gold
Σ		938				dk brown
♥		3021			◪	grey brown
◆		3371			◪	brown black
▣	Midnight	3750	◩	◪		dk blue
◈	Charm placement					

STITCH COUNT (73w x 84h)

14 count	5¼" x 6"
16 count	4⅝" x 5¼"
18 count	4⅛" x 4¾"
22 count	3⅜" x 3⅞"

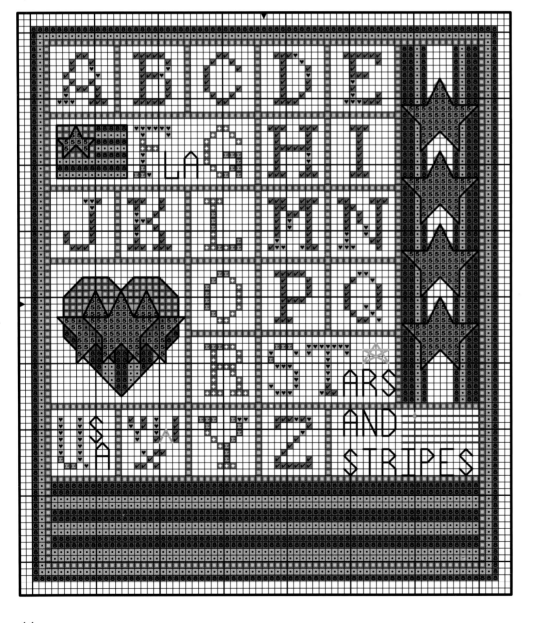

WOODLAND PEACE SAMPLER (shown on page 52, chart is on facing page) was stitched over 2 fabric threads on a 15" x 18" piece of Natural Irish Linen (28 ct). Two strands of floss were used for Cross Stitch and 1 strand for Backstitch. Design was custom framed.

Design by Polly Carbonari.

X	DMC	B'ST	COLOR
✚	666	◪	red

STITCH COUNT (98w x 141h)

14 count	7"	x 10⅛"
16 count	6⅛"	x 8⅞"
18 count	5½"	x 7⅞"
22 count	4½"	x 6½"

I knew by the smoke, that so gracefully curl'd
Above the green elms, that a cottage was near,
And I said, "If there's peace to be found in the world,
A heart that was humble might hope for it here!"
T. Moore

PEACE AND PLENTY (shown on page 53) was stitched over 2 fabric threads on a 14" × 20" piece of Zweigart® Light Mocha Cashel Linen® (28 ct). Two strands of floss were used for Cross Stitch and 1 strand for Backstitch.

Personalize and date design using DMC 989 floss and alphabet and numerals from chart. Design was custom framed.

Design by Deborah A. Lambein.

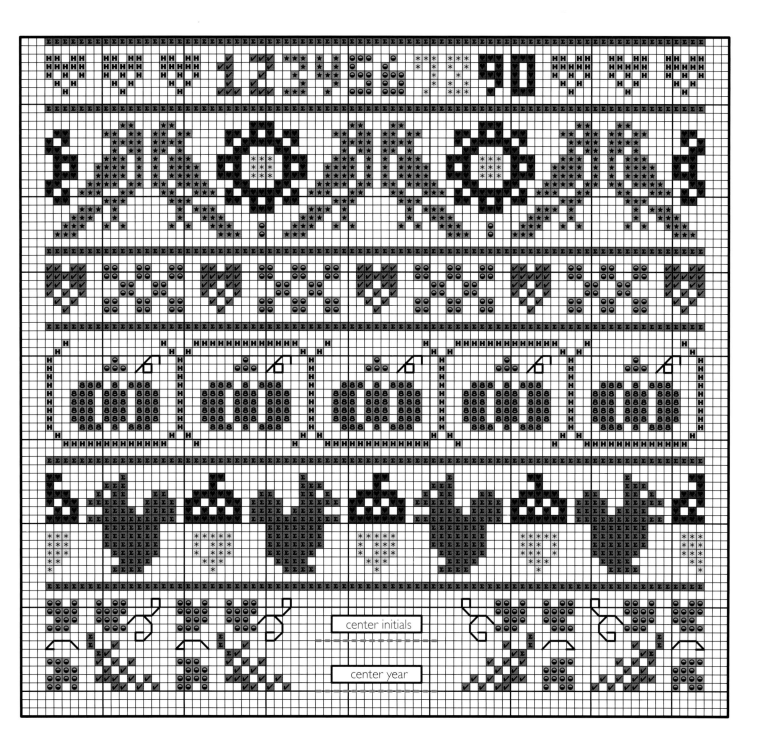

center initials

center year

X	DMC	B'ST	COLOR		X	DMC	B'ST	COLOR		STITCH COUNT (81w x 170h)	
★	312		blue		✳	781		gold		14 count	5⁷⁄₈" × 12¹⁄₄"
✔	327		purple		8	922		orange		16 count	5¹⁄₈" × 10⁵⁄₈"
♥	347		red		H	989		green		18 count	4¹⁄₂" × 9¹⁄₂"
Σ	433		brown		▨	Indicates first row of				22 count	3³⁄₄" × 7³⁄₄"
⊖	562	╱	dk green			bottom section of design.					

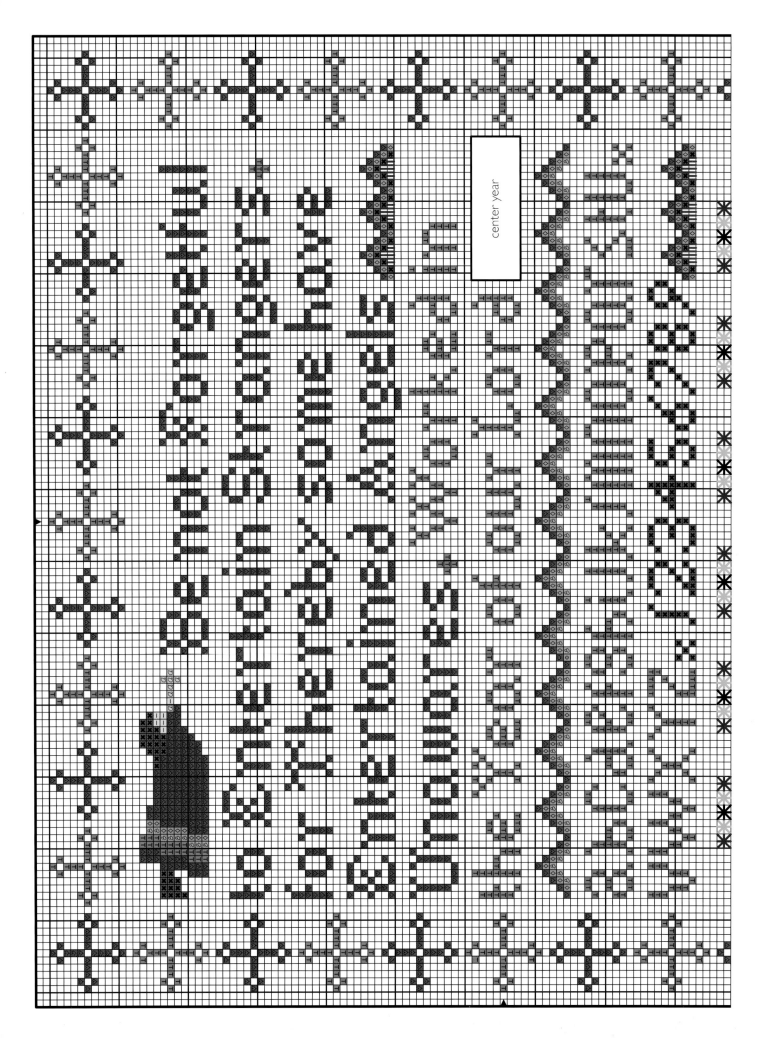

center year

center initials

ANGELS UNAWARES (shown on page 54) was stitched over 2 fabric threads on a 17" square of Zweigart® Cream Belfast Linen (32 ct). Two strands of floss were used for Cross Stitch and Smyrna Cross Stitch and 3 strands for Satin Stitch. Design was custom framed. Note: Aida fabric is not recommended for this design because of the Satin Stitches.

Design by Kandace Thomas.

STITCH DIAGRAMS

Smyrna Cross Stitch: Stitches 1-4 form the first Cross Stitch (**Fig. 1**). Stitches 5-8 form an upright Cross Stitch on top of the first Cross Stitch.

Satin Stitch: For Satin Stitches, follow **Fig. 2** to come up at odd numbers and go down at even numbers.

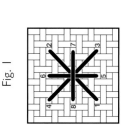

Fig. 2

Fig. 1

X	DMC	SMYRNA CROSS STITCH	SATIN STITCH	COLOR
▒	224	✳	✳	pink
I	225			lt pink
◇	501			green
a	680			gold
⊥	924	✳		blue green
▷	3726	✳	✳	dk pink
8	3782	✳		tan
✖	3787			brown

☑ Indicates last 2 rows of top section.

STITCH COUNT (131w x 131h)

14 count	9³/₈" × 9³/₈"
16 count	8¹/₄" × 8¹/₄"
18 count	7³/₈" × 7³/₈"

BOOKMARKS

Bookmarks are thoughtful little gifts! These designs, stitched on pre-finished or easy make-it-yourself bookmarks, cover a variety of hobbies and interests. Create a Bloom bookmark for your favorite gardener. Know someone who likes to read in bed? Stitch an Angel on Duty who'll stay nearby as he or she drifts off to sleep. A Bible verse, old-fashioned Sampler, or Vine design will appeal to plenty of people you know. Corner bookmarks slip onto a page to mark the progress of the reader.

Charts are on pages 76-77 and 80-81.

Charts on page 79.

Encourage the students and teachers in your life with the three Back to School Bookmarks. In floral lore, Violets are symbols of modesty and simplicity. The Celtic design on Dad's Keepsake Bookmark is fun to stitch. The same is true of the three Variegated Vine Bookmarks, which are all stitched from the same simple chart—the appearance changes when you use a different variegated floss color for each bookmark.

Charts are on pages 78-80.

X	DMC	1/4X	B'ST	COLOR
☆	blanc			white
❯	209			lavender
H	210			lt lavender
a	301			terra cotta
V	437			tan
▲	562			green
✔	563			lt green
3	597			turquoise
C	598			lt turquoise
◆	603			dk pink
4	604			pink
✳	738			lt tan
✕	743			yellow
✚	744			lt yellow
♡	761			lt pink
	783			gold
▲	840			dk taupe
n	841			taupe
−	948			peach
T	3072			grey
	3371			black brown
✕	3776			lt terra cotta
□	3838			blue
Z	3839			lt blue
●	3371			black brown Fr. Knot

ANGEL and BLOOM BOOKMARKS

(shown on page 72) were stitched on purchased white Aida bookmarks (18 ct). Two strands of floss were used for Cross Stitch and 1 strand for Backstitch and Fr. Knots. Design sizes are 1. 1½" × 6⅜" and 2. 1½" × 6⅜".

Designs by Deborah A. Lambein.

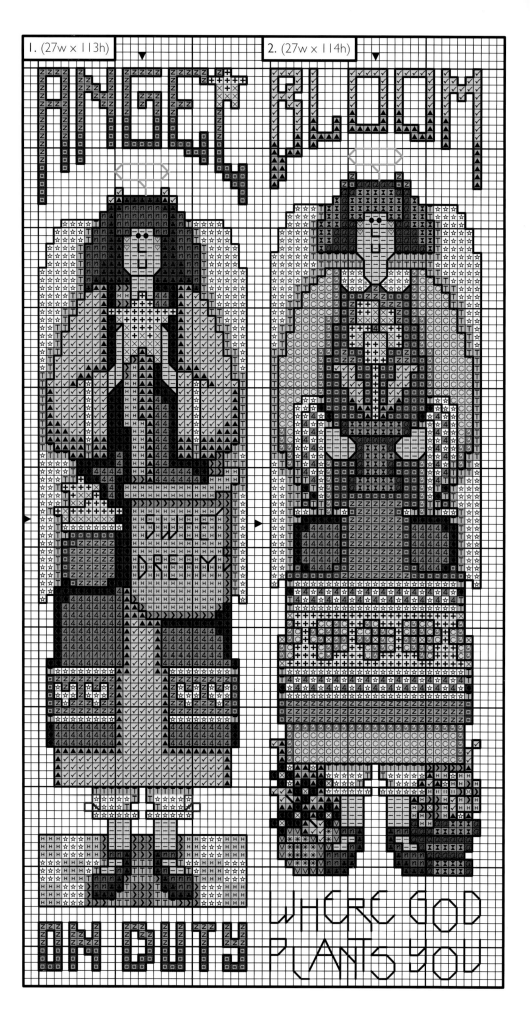

76 www.leisurearts.com

X	DMC	1/4X	B'ST	COLOR
•	blanc			white
■	319		/	vy dk green
◣	320			green
▶	326			cranberry
◆	335		/	dk pink
◉	340			violet
‖	341	•		lt violet
•	367	•	/	dk green
○	368		/	lt green
★	369	•	/	vy lt green
•	725	•		dk yellow
•	746			lt yellow
✕	818	•		vy lt pink
■	899		/	pink
□	938			dk brown
I	3078			yellow
■	3326			lt pink
✿	3746			dk violet
☆	3747			vy lt violet

FLORAL CORNER BOOKMARKS (shown on page 73) were each stitched on a purchased white Aida (18 ct) corner bookmark. Two strands of floss were used for Cross Stitch and 1 strand for Backstitch. Design sizes are 3. 4 1/8" x 2 1/4", 4. 3" x 2", and 5. 3 1/2" x 2 1/4".

Designs by Terrie Lee Steinmeyer.

3. (74w x 40h)

4. (53w x 36h)

5. (62w x 40h)

6.

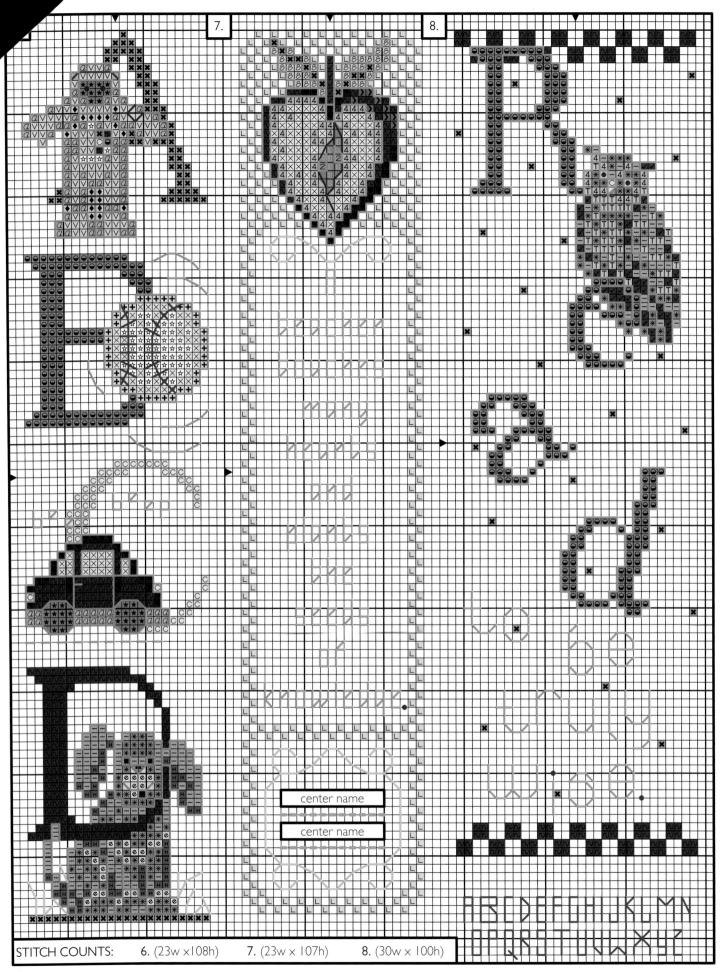

A teacher touches many hearts and plants the seeds of knowledge.

center name

center name

STITCH COUNTS: 6. (23w ×108h)   7. (23w × 107h)   8. (30w × 100h)

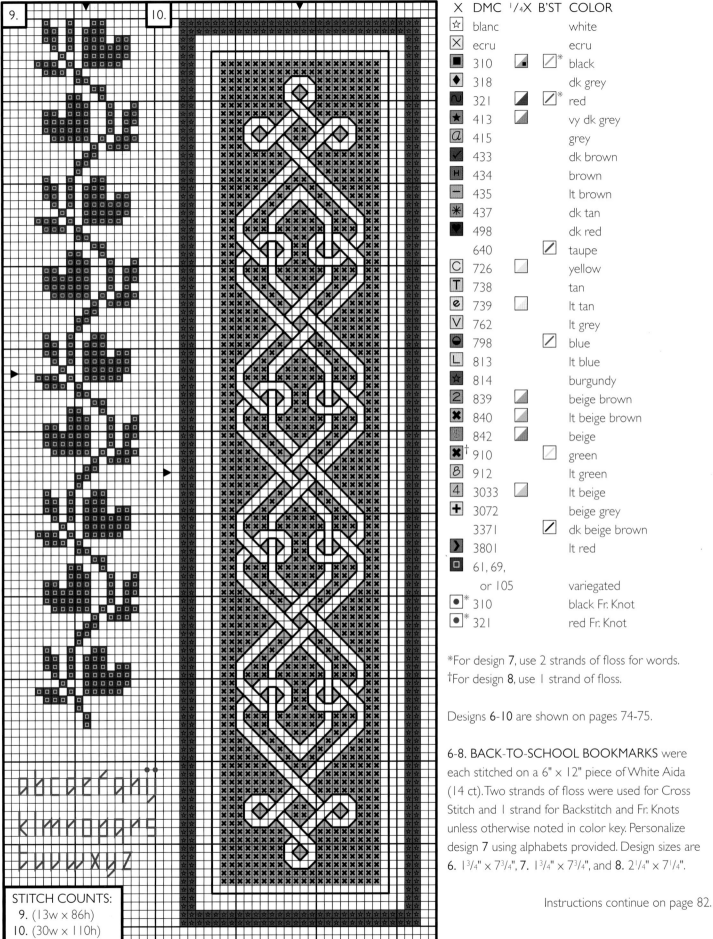

X	DMC	¼X	B'ST	COLOR
☆	blanc			white
☒	ecru			ecru
■	310	◩	◩*	black
◆	318			dk grey
N	321	◪	◩*	red
★	413			vy dk grey
ⓐ	415			grey
✔	433			dk brown
H	434			brown
—	435			lt brown
✱	437			dk tan
♥	498			dk red
	640		◪	taupe
C	726	◪		yellow
T	738			tan
e	739	◪		lt tan
V	762			lt grey
◒	798		◪	blue
L	813			lt blue
☆	814			burgundy
2	839	◪		beige brown
✖	840	◪		lt beige brown
$	842	◪		beige
✖†	910	◪		green
8	912			lt green
4	3033	◪		lt beige
+	3072			beige grey
	3371		◪	dk beige brown
❭	3801			lt red
▣	61, 69,			
	or 105			variegated
⬤*	310			black Fr. Knot
⬤*	321			red Fr. Knot

*For design **7**, use 2 strands of floss for words.
†For design **8**, use 1 strand of floss.

Designs **6-10** are shown on pages 74-75.

6-8. BACK-TO-SCHOOL BOOKMARKS were each stitched on a 6" x 12" piece of White Aida (14 ct). Two strands of floss were used for Cross Stitch and 1 strand for Backstitch and Fr. Knots unless otherwise noted in color key. Personalize design **7** using alphabets provided. Design sizes are 6. 1¾" x 7¾", 7. 1¾" x 7¾", and 8. 2¼" x 7¼".

Instructions continue on page 82.

STITCH COUNTS:
9. (13w x 86h)
10. (30w x 110h)

X	DMC	¼X	B'ST	COLOR
☆	blanc			white
	315		✦	vy dk mauve
♡	316			mauve
$	319			dk green
⬥	320			lt green
▼	367			green
U	368			vy lt green
⬚	500			dk blue green
Z	501			blue green
3	502		✦	lt blue green
C	503			vy lt blue green
⊠	524	◪		lt olive
I	610	◪	✦	dk brown
n	611	◪		brown
V	613	◪		lt brown
	646		✦	dk grey
−	648	◪		grey
✚	676			yellow
✕	729			dk yellow
4	778			vy lt mauve
e*	3041 &			violet &
	340			lt purple
◼	3042			lt violet
◼	3045	◪		gold
◉	3046			lt gold
✳	3051	◪		dk olive
⬒	3052	◪		olive
T	3072	◪		lt grey
✓	3348	◪		yellow green
	3362		✦	dk pine
#	3363	◪		pine
∞	3364	◪		lt pine
★	3685			burgundy
◆	3726			dk mauve
n	3727	◪		lt mauve
	3740		✦	dk violet
❭*	3740 &			dk violet &
	3746			purple
H	3743	◪		vy lt violet

*Blended floss. Use 1 strand of each color listed.

Designs 11-13 are shown on pages 73-74.

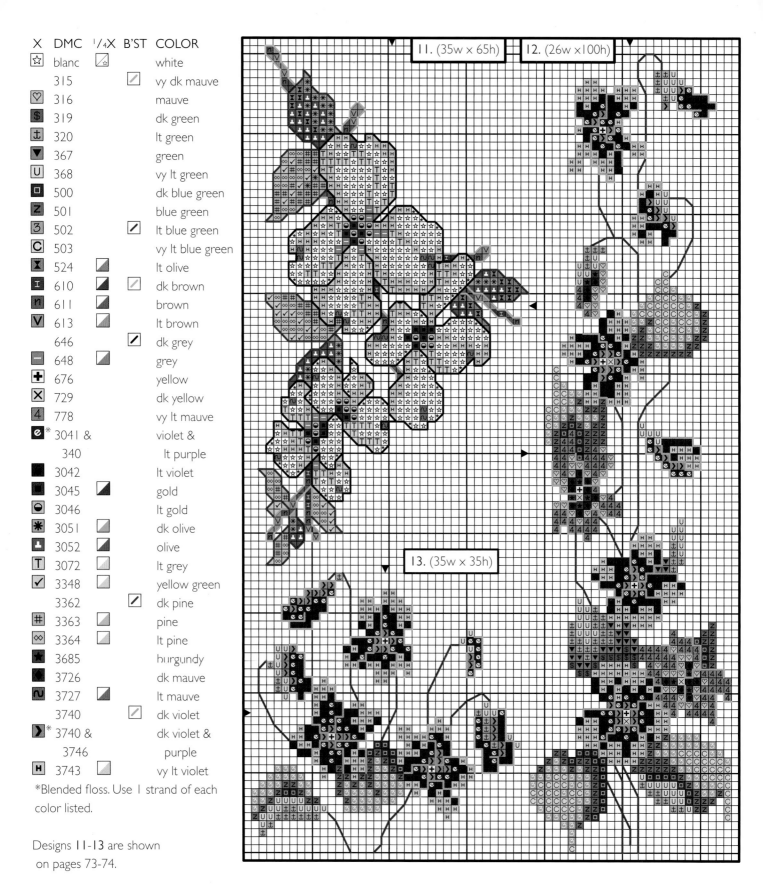

11. (35w x 65h) 12. (26w x100h)

13. (35w x 35h)

11. DOGWOOD BLOSSOMS CORNER BOOKMARK was stitched on a purchased White Aida (18 ct) corner bookmark. Two strands of floss were used for Cross Stitch and 1 strand for Backstitch. Design size is 3⅝" × 2".

Design by Donna Vermillion Giampa.

12. VIOLETS FRINGED BOOKMARK was stitched over 2 fabric threads on an 8" × 12" piece of Zweigart® Antique White Belfast Linen (32 ct) using 2 strands of floss for Cross Stitch and 1 strand for Backstitch. Design size is 1⅝" × 6¼".

Instructions continue on page 82.

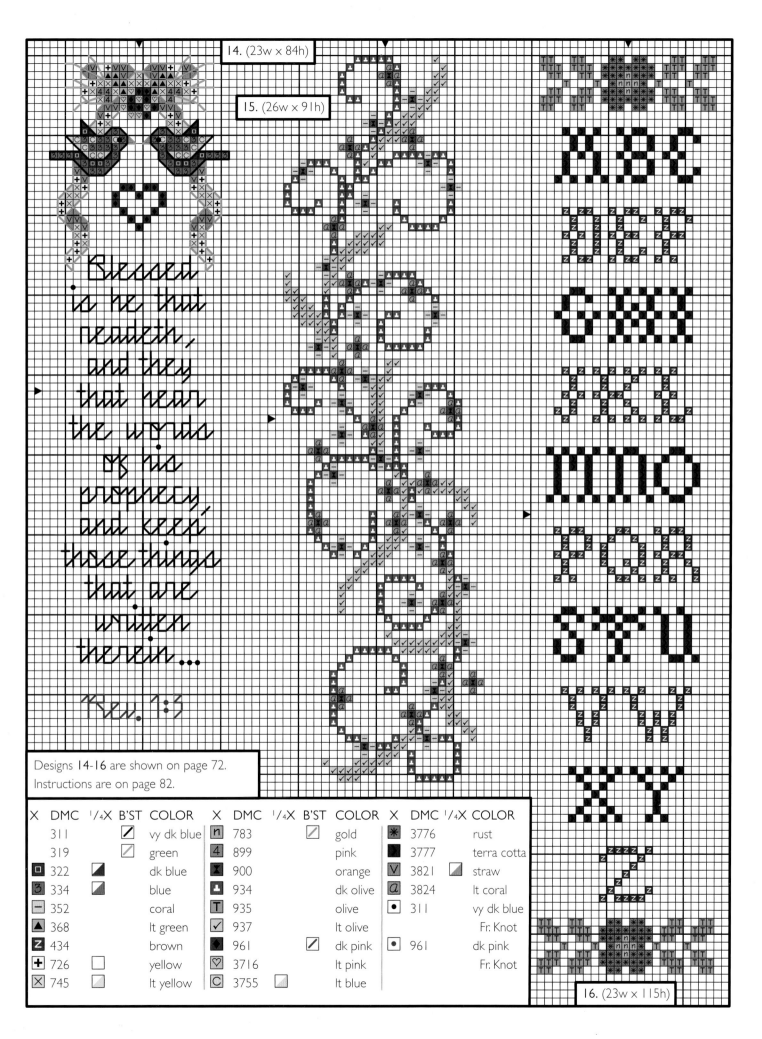

14. (23w × 84h)

15. (26w × 91h)

Blessed is he that readeth, and they that hear the words of his prophecy, and keep those things that are written therein...

Rev. 1:3

Designs 14-16 are shown on page 72.
Instructions are on page 82.

X	DMC	¹/₄X	B'ST	COLOR	X	DMC	¹/₄X	B'ST	COLOR	X	DMC	¹/₄X	COLOR
	311		◢	vy dk blue	n	783		◢	gold	✳	3776		rust
	319		◢	green	4	899			pink	■	3777		terra cotta
◻	322	◢		dk blue	✕	900			orange	V	3821	◢	straw
3	334	◢		blue	♣	934			dk olive	a	3824		lt coral
−	352			coral	T	935			olive	●	311		vy dk blue
▲	368			lt green	✓	937			lt olive				Fr. Knot
Z	434			brown	◆	961		◢	dk pink	●	961		dk pink
✚	726			yellow	♡	3716			lt pink				Fr. Knot
✕	745	◩		lt yellow	C	3755	◩		lt blue				

16. (23w × 115h)

6-8. BACK-TO-SCHOOL BOOKMARKS (continued from page 79). For bookmark, center design and trim fabric to $^3/_4$" larger than design on all sides. Machine stitch across short edges $^1/_2$" from edges. Fringe short edges by removing one horizontal thread at a time to one square from stitching line. Press each long edge $^1/_4$" to wrong side, press $^1/_4$" to wrong side again, and hem.

Designs by Jane Chandler.

9. VARIEGATED VINE BOOKMARK (chart is on page 79) was stitched 3 times on purchased Ecru Aida (14 ct) bookmarks. Shown left to right in photo are DMC variegated floss numbers 61, 105, and 69. Three strands of floss were used for Cross Stitch. To achieve subtle shading, cross each stitch individually as you work across the row. Design size is 1" x 6$^1/_4$".

Design by Karin Miller.

10. DAD'S KEEPSAKE BOOKMARK (chart is on page 79) was stitched on a 6" x 10" piece of Ivory Aida (18 ct) using 2 strands of floss for Cross Stitch and 1 strand for Backstitch. Design size is 1$^3/_4$" x 6$^1/_8$".

For bookmark, you will need a 13" length of 1"w grosgrain ribbon. Centering design, trim stitched piece to 3" x 7$^3/_8$". Press each long edge $^1/_4$" to wrong side, press $^1/_4$" to wrong side again, and hem. Repeat for each short edge. Fold one end of ribbon 3" to front; glue in place. Referring to photo, glue wrong side of bookmark to front of ribbon. Trim end of ribbon as desired.

Design by Ann Gunn Everitt.

12. VIOLETS FRINGED BOOKMARK (continued from page 80). For bookmark, you will need blanc DMC Pearl Cotton #12. Work Nun Stitch (see lower right corner, this page) $^1/_2$" from edge of design on all sides; trim fabric close to Nun Stitch on long edges. Trim 1$^3/_4$" from Nun Stitch on short edges; fringe to Nun Stitch.

Design by Linda Culp Calhoun.

13. VIOLETS RIBBON BOOKMARK (chart is on page 80) was stitched over 2 fabric threads on an 8" square of Zweigart® Antique White Belfast Linen (32 ct) using 2 strands of floss for Cross Stitch and 1 strand for Backstitch. Design size is 2$^1/_4$" x 2$^1/_4$".

For bookmark, you will need blanc DMC Pearl Cotton #12, 13" length of 1"w ribbon, 13" length of $^3/_8$"w ribbon, and craft glue. Work Nun Stitch (see lower right corner, this page) $^1/_4$" from edge of design on all sides; trim fabric close to Nun Stitch. Center and glue wrong side of $^3/_8$"w ribbon to right side of 1"w ribbon; allow glue to dry. Fold one short edge of ribbons 1$^1/_2$" to wrong side; glue in place. Trim remaining short edge diagonally. Refer to photo and glue stitched piece 1$^1/_4$" from folded edge.

Design by Linda Culp Calhoun.

14. REVELATIONS 1:3 BOOKMARK (chart is on page 81) was stitched on a purchased White Aida bookmark (14 ct). Three strands of floss were used for Cross Stitch and 1 strand for Backstitch. Design size is 1$^3/_4$" x 6".

Design by Jane Chandler.

15. VINE BOOKMARK (chart is on page 81) was stitched over 2 fabric threads on a 7$^1/_2$" x 12$^1/_2$" piece of Natural Linen (32 ct) using 2 strands of floss for Cross Stitch. Design size is 1$^5/_8$" x 5$^3/_4$".

For bookmark, center design and trim fabric to 3$^1/_4$" x 8$^1/_2$". Machine stitch across short edges $^3/_4$" from edges. Fringe short edges by removing 1 horizontal thread at a time to 1 square from stitching line. Press each long edge $^1/_4$" to wrong side, press $^1/_4$" to wrong side again, and hem.

Design by Judy Chrispens.

16. SAMPLER BOOKMARK (chart is on page 81) was stitched over 2 fabric threads on a 7" x 13$^1/_2$" piece of Zweigart® Antique Ivory Cashel Linen® (28 ct) using 3 strands of floss for Cross Stitch. Design size is 1$^3/_4$" x 8$^1/_4$".

For bookmark, center design and trim fabric to 3" x 9$^1/_2$". Machine stitch across short edges $^3/_8$" from edges. Fringe short edges by removing 1 horizontal thread at a time to 1 square from stitching line. Press each long edge $^1/_4$" to wrong side, press $^1/_4$" to wrong side again, and hem.

Design by Diane Williams.

NUN STITCH

This continuous edging stitch is worked from top to bottom. Each stitch is worked twice; stitches 1-2 and 3-4 are over the same fabric threads (**Fig. 1**). Come up at 1 and pull tightly toward 2, then go down at 2 and pull tightly toward 1. In the same manner, work stitch 3-4 over the same fabric threads. Work stitches 5-16 in the same manner (**Fig. 1**). Continue working to corner, ending with a stitch worked as 13-16. To turn corner, come up at 17 and then go down at 18. Work stitch 19-20 over the same fabric threads (**Fig. 2**). Turn fabric 90° to the right; work stitches 21-24 (**Fig. 3**). Continue working around edges, keeping tension even.

Fig. 1   Fig. 2   Fig 3.

ALPHABETS

One of the many fun things about Cross Stitch is the way it allows you to express yourself. These thirty-nine alphabets are your opportunity to personalize your projects with your initials, monogram a gift, or simply say something fun in stitches. We've included a word stitched from each set of letters so you can see how they will look on fabric.

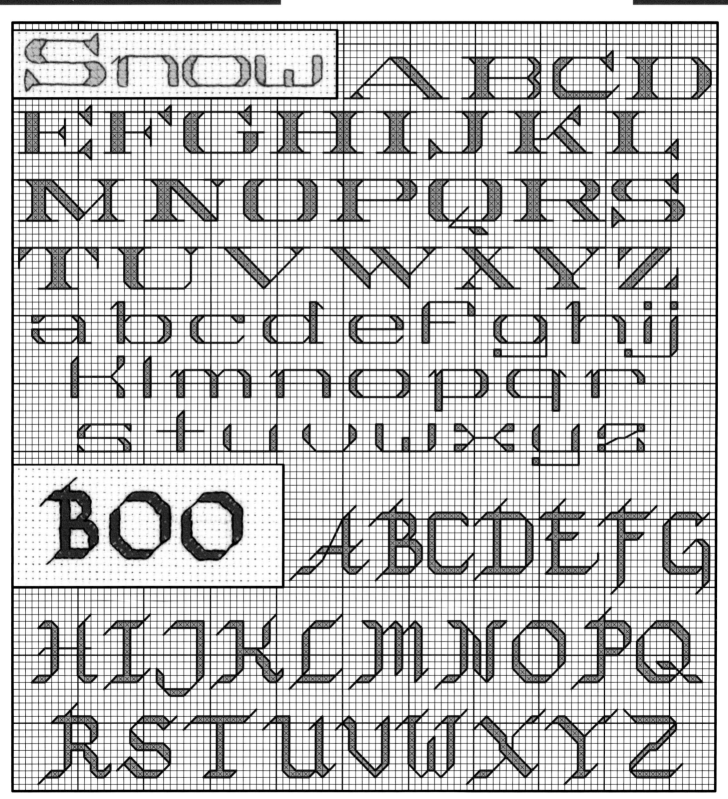

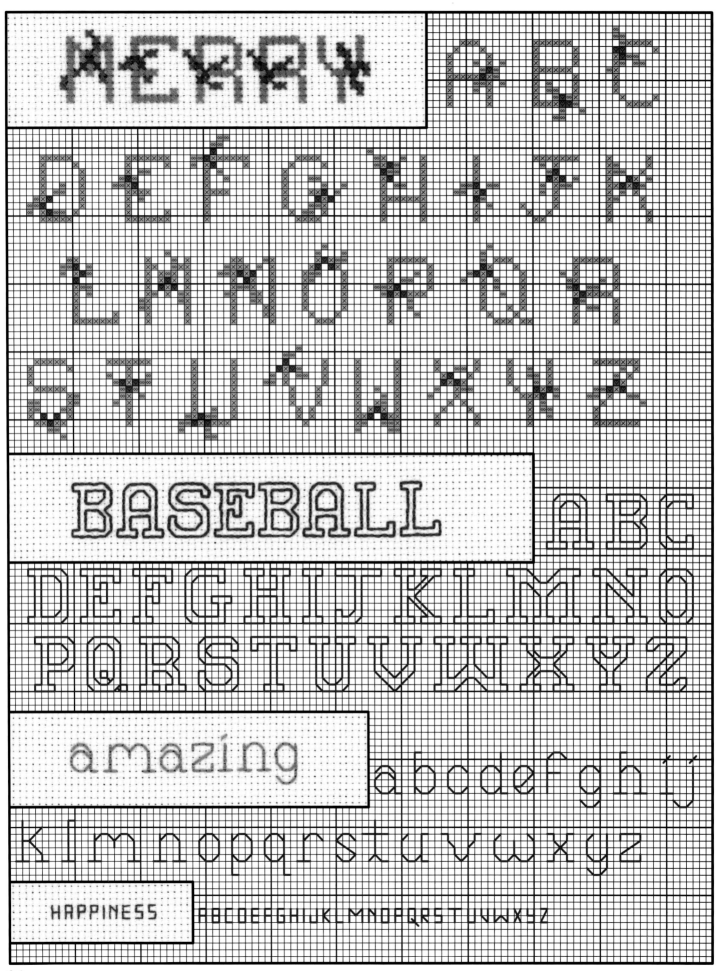

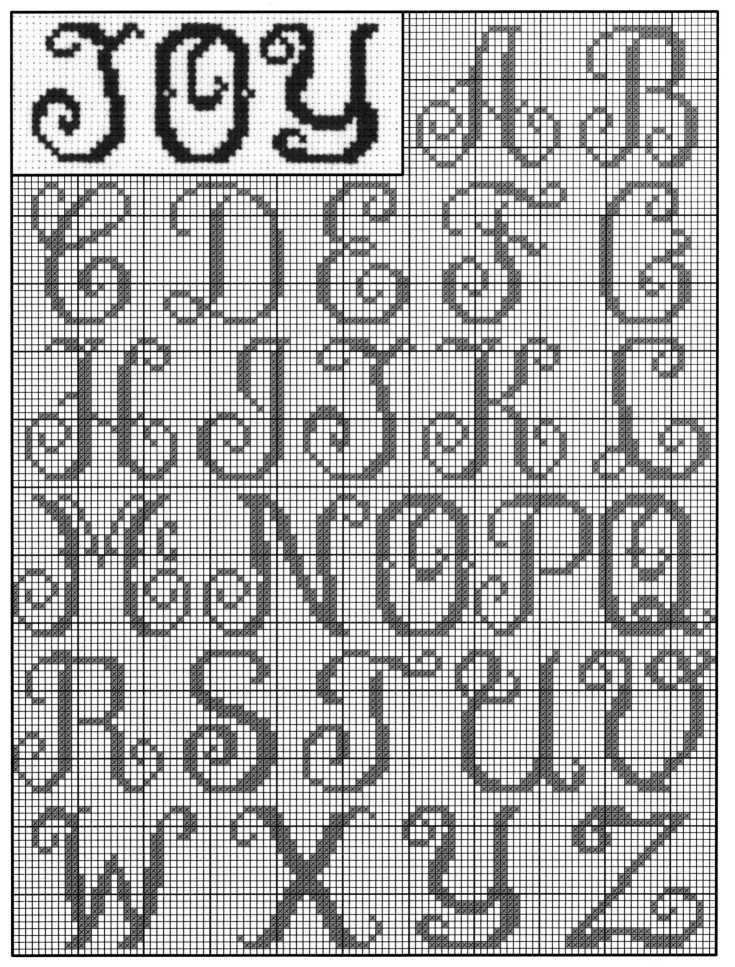

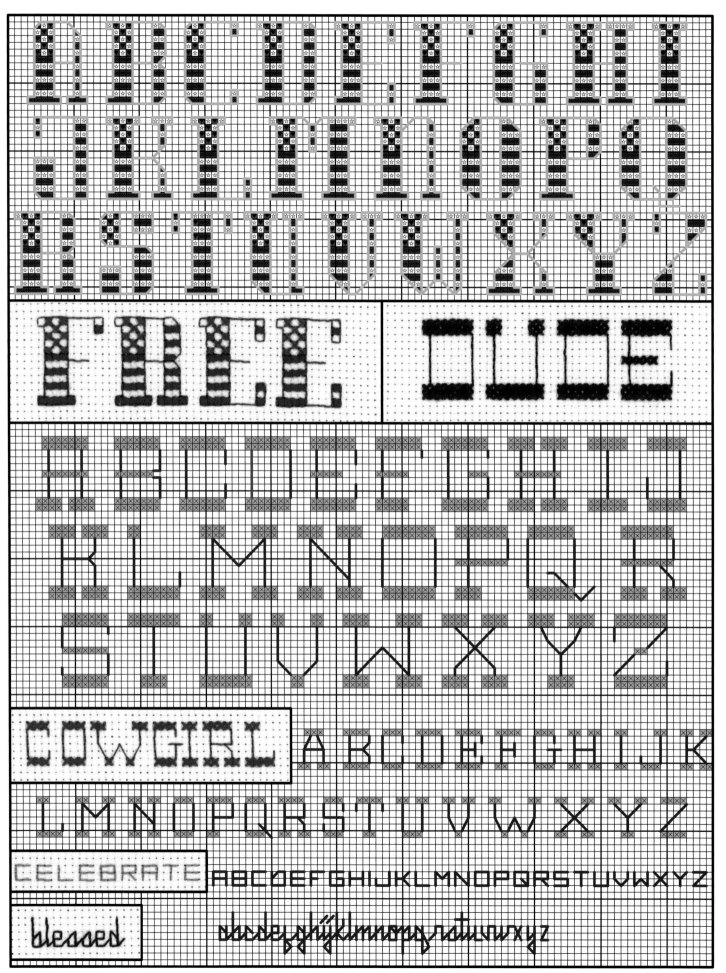

Bloom abcdefghijk
lmnopqrstuvwxyz

ABCDEFGHI
JKLMNOPQR
STUVWXYZ

hello abcdef
ghijklmnopq
rstuvwxyz

Peace ABCDEFGHIJKLM
NOPQRSTUVWXYZ abcd
efghijklmnopqrstuvwxyz

LOVE

A B C D E F G
H I J K L M N O P Q
R S T U V W X Y Z

Memories

A B C D E F G H I J K
L M N O P Q R S T U V W X Y Z

a b c d e f g h i j k l m n o p q r s t u v w x y z

smile

a b c d e f g h i j k l
m n o p q r s t u v w x y z

Family

A B C D E F G H I J K L M
N O P Q R S T U V W X Y Z
a b c d e f g h i j k l m n o p q r s t u v w x y z

cherish a b c d e f g h i j k l m n o p q r s t u v w x y z

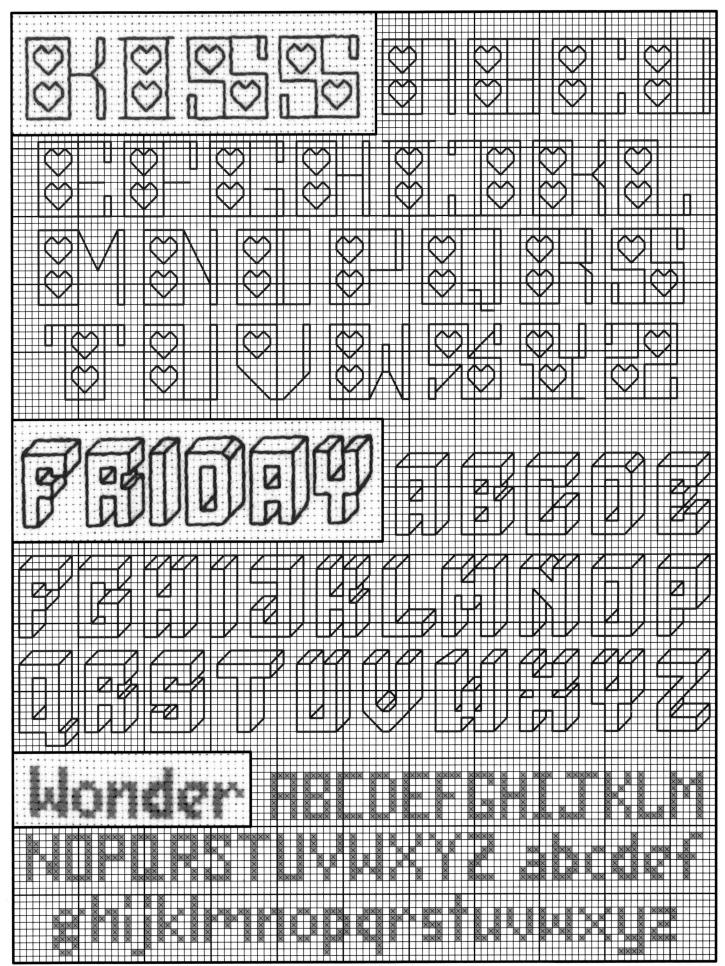

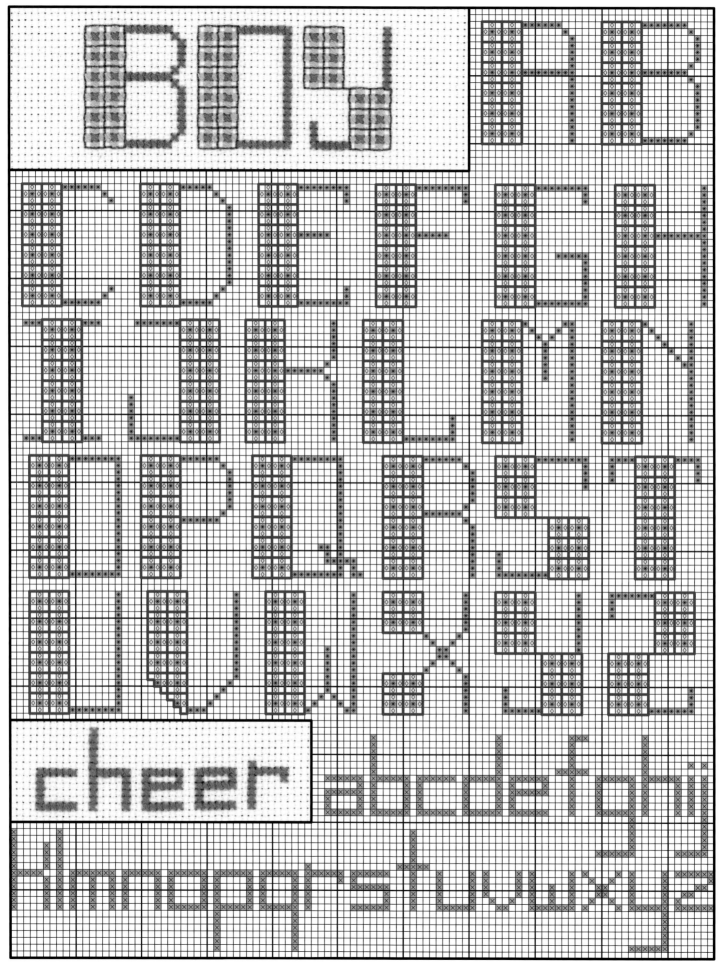

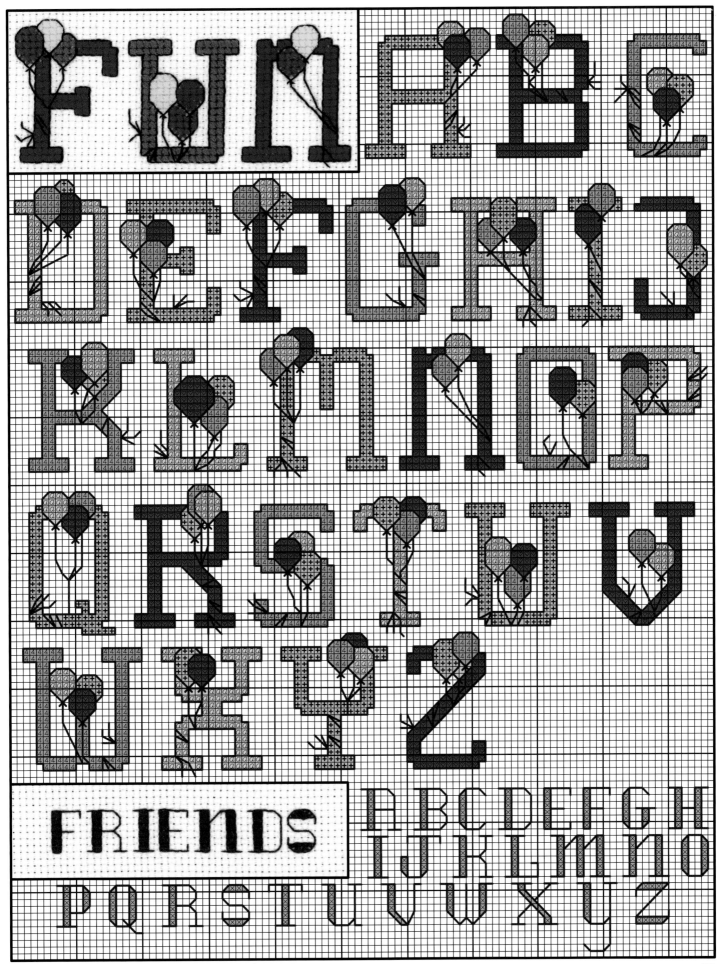

GENERAL INSTRUCTIONS

HOW TO READ CHARTS

Each chart is made up of a key and a gridded design where each square represents a stitch. The symbols in the key tell which floss color to use for each stitch in the chart. The following headings and symbols are given:

> X – Cross Stitch
> DMC – DMC color number
> ¹/₄X – One-Quarter Stitch
> ¹/₂X – Half Cross Stitch
> ³/₄X – Three-Quarter Stitch
> B'ST – Backstitch
> COLOR – The name given to the floss color
>   in this chart

A square filled with a color and a symbol should be worked as a **Cross Stitch**, unless a **Half Cross Stitch** is indicated in color key.

A triangle filled with color and/or a symbol should be worked as a **Quarter Stitch**.

A straight line should be worked as a **Backstitch**.

A large dot listed near the end of the key should be worked as a **French Knot** (abbreviated as **Fr. Knot**).

A loop listed near the end of the key should be worked as a **Lazy Daisy Stitch**.

In the chart, the symbol for a **Cross Stitch** may be omitted when a **Backstitch** crosses its square.

HOW TO STITCH

Always work **Cross Stitches**, **Half Cross Stitches**, and **Quarter Stitches** first and then add the **Backstitch**, **French Knots**, **Lazy Daisy Stitches**, and any **Special Stitches**.

Cross Stitch (X): For horizontal rows, work stitches in two journeys (**Fig. 1**). For vertical rows, complete each stitch as shown (**Fig. 2**). When working over 2 fabric threads, work **Cross Stitch** as shown in **Fig. 3**.

Fig. 1   Fig. 2

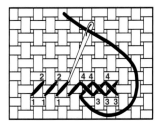

Fig. 3

Half Cross Stitch (¹/₂X): This stitch is one journey of the Cross Stitch and is worked from lower left to upper right as shown (**Fig. 4**). When working over 2 fabric threads, work **Half Cross Stitch** as shown in **Fig. 5**.

Fig. 4   Fig. 5

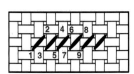
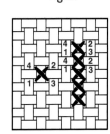

Quarter Stitch (¼X and ¾X): Come up at 1, then split fabric to go down at 2 (**Fig. 6**). When stitches 1-4 are worked in the same color, the resulting stitch is called a **Three-Quarter Stitch** (¾X) (**Fig. 7**). When working over 2 fabric threads, work Quarter Stitches as shown in **Fig. 8**.

Fig. 6

Fig. 7

Fig. 8

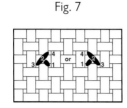

Backstitch (B'ST): For outlines and details, Backstitch should be worked after the design has been completed (**Fig. 9**). When working over two fabric threads, work Backstitch as shown in Fig. 10.

Fig. 9

Fig. 10

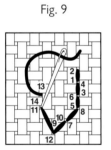

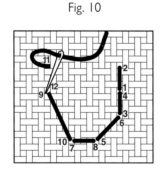

French Knot (Fr. Knot): Bring needle up at 1. Wrap floss once around needle. Insert needle at 2, tighten knot, and pull needle through fabric, holding floss until it must be released (**Fig. 11**). For a larger knot, use more floss strands; wrap only once.

Fig. 11

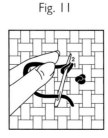

Lazy Daisy Stitch: Bring needle up at 1 and make a loop. Go back down at 1 and come up at 2, keeping floss below point of needle (**Fig. 12**). Pull needle through and go down at 3 to anchor loop, completing stitch. (To support stitches, it may be helpful to go down in edge of next fabric thread when anchoring loop.)

Fig. 12

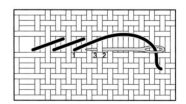

Algerian Eye Stitch: Come up at 1 and all odd numbers; go down in center (**Fig. 13**).

Fig. 13

Outline Stitch: Working in channel created by removed thread, come up at 1; go down at 2. Come up at 3, keeping point of needle below floss (**Fig. 14**).

Fig. 14

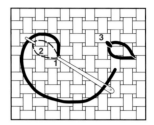

Satin Stitch: Come up at 1 and all odd numbers and go down at 2 and all even numbers (**Fig. 15**).

Fig. 15

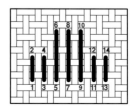

Working over Two Fabric Threads

Use the sewing method instead of the stab method when working over two fabric threads. To use the sewing method, keep your stitching hand on the right side of fabric (instead of stabbing the fabric with the needle and taking your stitching hand to the back of the fabric to pick up the needle). With the sewing method, you take the needle down and up with one stroke instead of two. To add support to stitches, it is important that the first cross stitch is place on the fabric with stitch 1–2 beginning and ending where a vertical fabric thread crosses over a horizontal fabric thread (**Fig. 16**). When the first stitch is in the correct position, the entire design will be placed properly, with vertical fabric threads supporting each stitch.

Fig. 16

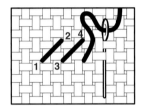

STITCHING YOUR DESIGN

Figuring the Size to Cut Fabric

Most projects include the size to cut fabric if you are making the project as shown in photograph; however, you may wish to use a fabric with a different stitch count, or finish your design in another manner. To determine size of fabric needed, follow the steps below.

1. Count the squares in the width of your design.
2. Divide that number by the thread count of your fabric. This gives you the width of your design in inches when stitched on the particular count fabric.

Examples

70 squares wide ÷ 14 count Aida = 5" wide

70 squares wide ÷ 32 count linen worked over 2 threads (or 16) = $4^3/_8$" wide

3. Repeat the process to find the height of the design.
4. When cutting fabric, add at least 3" to each side of larger designs and at least 2" to smaller designs.

Using the Right Number Of Floss Strands

The table below gives the recommended number of floss strands for common fabric thread counts.

Thread Count per inch	Number of Strands for Cross Stitch	Number of Strands for Backstitch	Number of Strands for French Knot
8.5	6	2	4
10 or 11	4 or 5	2	3
12 or 13	3	1	2
14	2 or 3	1	1 or 2
16	2	1	1
18	2	1	1
22	1	1	1

ASSEMBLY AND FINISHING TECHNIQUES

Needle Case Assembly

1. For outline stitch border, measure 2" from each raw edge of fabric and pull (remove) 1 fabric thread. Using 4 strands of floss (DMC 725 for yellow, DMC 3712 for pink, DMC 340 for purple) and beginning in one corner, work an Outline Stitch (**Fig. 14**, page 94) rectangular border in pulled thread areas. Fold fabric in half matching short edges. With folded edge on left, center and stitch design (inside the border) on rectangle half.

2. Cut a $7^7/_8$" × $3^7/_8$" piece of fusible interfacing. Center and fuse interfacing to wrong side of stitched piece. Trim stitched piece $1/_2$" from Outline Stitches. Press edges to wrong side along Outline Stitches. Cut a 9" × 5" lining fabric piece; press edges $1/_2$" to wrong side. Matching wrong sides and folded edges, whipstitch lining to stitched piece. Cut a 7" × 3" felt piece. Matching short edges, fold felt in half; mark center. Matching short edges, fold stitched piece and attached lining in half; mark center of lining. Matching center of felt to center of lining, use white thread to machine sew through all thicknesses along center line.

3. For each twisted cord tie, cut a 40" length of 6 strands of floss (same color as Outline Stitch). Fold floss in half and knot ends together. Use a small crochet hook to pull loop of floss through needle case at center of one short edge, pulling until knot meets needle case. Insert finger through loop of floss and twist until floss is tight on finger. Match knot and loop ends of floss, sliding needle case to center of floss. Holding floss so that it will not untwist, remove finger and knot ends together. Slowly release floss, guiding it so that it twists evenly. Trim ends near knot. Repeat for other side of needle case.

Pillow Finishing

Note: Instructions provided here include adding cording and a ruffle. You may add either or both to your pillow. Use a 1/2" seam and match right sides throughout unless noted.

1. For pillow front, trim stitched piece to desired size plus 1/2" on all sides for seam allowances. Cut pillow back same size as pillow front.

2. To make cording, measure edges of pillow front and add 4"; cut a 2 1/2"w bias strip of fabric this measurement, piecing as needed. Center 1/4" diameter cord on wrong side of bias strip. Matching wrong sides and long edges, fold bias strip over cord. Using zipper foot, baste close to cord. Trim seam allowances to 1/2". Matching raw edges and beginning and ending 3" from ends of cording, baste cording to right side of pillow front. To make turning corners easier, clip seam allowances of cording at pillow corners. Remove approximately 3" of seam at one end of cording; fold bias strip away from cord. Trim remaining end of cording so that cord ends meet exactly. Fold end of loose bias strip 1/2" to wrong side; fold bias strip back over area where ends meet. Baste remainder of cording to pillow front.

3. To determine width of folded ruffle, such as on Floral Fancy and Blue Blossoms (page 18), multiply desired finished ruffle width by 2 and add 1" for seam allowances. To determine length of ruffle, measure edges of pillow front and multiply by 2. To make ruffle, cut fabric strip the determined measurements, piecing as needed. Sew short edges together to form a large ring; press seam allowances open. Fold ring along length with wrong sides together and raw edges matching; press.

4. To determine width of single thickness ruffle, such as the ruffle on Spring Finesse (page 21), add 1" to desired finished ruffle width. To determine length of ruffle, measure edges of pillow front and multiply by 2. Cut a fabric strip the determined measurements, piecing as needed. Sew short edges together to form a large ring; press seam allowances open. Press one long edge 1/4" to wrong side twice and hem.

5. To gather ruffle, baste 1/4" and 3/8" from raw edge. Pull basting threads, gathering ruffle to fit pillow front. Matching raw edges, baste ruffle to right side of pillow front. With right sides together and using 1/2" seam allowance (or stitching as close as possible to cording), sew pillow front and back together, leaving an opening at bottom edge for turning.

6. Turn pillow right side out, carefully pushing corners outward. Stuff with polyester fiberfill and sew opening closed.

7. For pillow with trim, such as Zinnias (page 25), sew pillow front and back together, leaving an opening at bottom edge for turning. Turn pillow right side out, carefully pushing corners outward. Stuff with polyester fiberfill and sew opening closed. Hand stitch trim around edges of pillow.

WHERE TO FIND IT

The following are some of the products available at www.TheLeisureBoutique.com:

- 11, 14, 16, and 18 count Aida
- 22 count Hardanger
- 28 count Monaco
- 28 count Linen
- 14 and 18 count bookmarks
- fingertip and hand towels
- infant and toddler bibs

Other items may be found at your local craft store or through online retailers.

Some fabrics and pre-finished items provided courtesy of Charles Craft, Inc., and Zweigart®.
Embroidery floss provided courtesy of the DMC Corporation.